Everything Is Going to Be OK

EVERYTHING IS GOING TO BE

OK

A REAL TALK GUIDE
TO LIVING WELL WITH MENTAL ILLNESS

ASHLEY WOMBLE, MPH

Magical Thinking Media

New York

First Printing, 2018

ISBN-13: 978-0-6921-5598-1

For more information, visit www.ashleyawomble.com.

Book design by Lauren Harms

Note to the reader:

While this book provides general information about certain potential medical conditions in an accessible way, nothing in it should be considered medical advice and it is not intended in any way to be a substitute for professional medical advice, diagnosis, or treatment. Always seek the advice of your physician, therapist or another qualified health provider with any questions you may have regarding a diagnosed or suspected medical condition. Under no circumstances should you disregard professional medical advice or delay in seeking it because of something you have read in this book. You should not begin, stop, or alter an existing treatment plan that your doctor or therapist has established, based on anything you have read in this book without first consulting your doctor, therapist, or an appropriate medical professional.

Some names have been changed to protect privacy.

Special thanks to Dr. Ben Nordstrom and Dr. John Draper for reviewing.

For Barry, who has turned my nightmares into dreams, and dreams into reality

Contents

Part Eight: When It's Not You, It's…

Part Nine: Save Your Own Life

Part Ten: Resources

One Last Thing

Acknowledgments

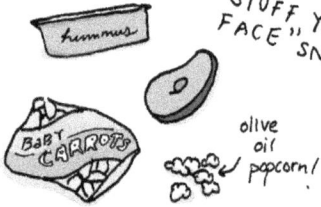

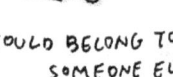

INTRODUCTION

If you're struggling with your mental health, someone has probably already promised you that "Everything is going to be OK." That little white lie is the easiest thing for people to say when they have no idea how things are going to turn out. "Everything is going to be OK" is empty. Some people even have the nerve to add with a smile, "If it isn't OK, then it isn't the end." It is not exactly helpful when you are pretty sure that things are going to get a hell of a lot worse. People say, "Everything is going to be OK" when what they really mean is, "I can't believe you are going through this and I'm scared." The truth is if you just wait around thinking everything will eventually be OK, your mental health will probably deteriorate.

Before I get to the how and why know this: You are so not alone. One-in-five people experience a mental illness at some point in his or her life. Most of us—make that seventy-five percent—start to feel it coming on before we turn twenty-four. Sometimes it's obvious that something is wrong, but it still might take years before you figure out exactly what's going on. Before you even know what hit you, the symptoms of mental illness can mess up your social life, education, and career. Life is hard enough. Trying to get your shit together when you aren't feeling mentally healthy is a real struggle.

Here's the good news: You actually have the power to *make* everything OK. It will take some time, support from the right people and professionals, and lots of love for and patience with yourself, but you can do this.

How This Book Will Help You

Throughout my personal and professional life (more on me later), I've learned that you can have a mental illness and live a happy and healthy life. You just need the right care and support. It's finding that support and paying for it that often trips people up. This is a book of information and advice—not doctor's orders—designed to help you to take control of your health, your life, and your future.

After consulting the leading books on mental illness, diving into clinical research, conducting interviews with people actually dealing with these issues, and surveying hundreds of young adults, I've come up with an action plan to help you save your own life. (You'll find out more about what people think about their mental health in the Real Talk survey results throughout the book.)

The book starts with what you didn't learn in psychology class about mental illness. In part one, I zero in on the symptoms of the most common mental disorders that young adults deal with and highlight stories of some who made their way to recovery. Part two is about therapies and medications that have been proven effective to treat those mental disorders—and perhaps more importantly, how to find a mental health professional you'll feel comfortable with. And, because health care is so freaking expensive, part three explains how you can pay for it on your budget.

In parts four and five I talk about how you can optimize your lifestyle and relationships to stay mentally healthy. Part six will help you navigate school and work so that you can spend your time focused on your purpose, not your diagnosis. Sometimes you get knocked down, so part seven offers inspiration from those who have already handled those "worst-case scenarios," such as getting sent to a mental hospital.

Maybe you aren't reading this book because of your mental health, but because you know someone who is dealing with a disorder. If that's what's going on, part eight explains how to help that person get better without being a jerk or compromising your own sanity.

One of the worst-case scenarios you may have dealt with—like a lot of us—is thinking about ending your life. It's essential for you to know that you aren't alone in this. You don't have to give those thoughts any power. Part nine is meant to prepare you to deal with suicidal thoughts and connect you with people who are standing by to help you right now. Part ten is a treasure chest of resources, including a state-by-state guide of government agencies and support groups, to help you get the support you need, wherever you are.

WHY AM I WRITING THIS?

In my own life, I've gone from dealing with depression, anxiety, suicidal thoughts, and shitloads of grief to being ridiculously happy. But, like pretty much everyone, I didn't know anything about mental illness until it showed up on my doorstep.

When I was in my twenties, my life looked like a rom-com. Career-wise, I had "made it." I was an editor for *Cosmopolitan*, where I got paid to write jokes about celebrities wearing terrible outfits, interview authors I admired, and regularly chat up male models. It was as glamorous as it sounds, and I got all the free beauty products I could ever want. I even lived in Brooklyn with a quirky roommate who looked a bit like Zooey Deschanel.

Everything was perfect, except for me. Smiling at work felt like a job in itself. Even though I always seemed to have plans for happy hour, or some guy to crush on, I really just wanted to be alone. When I drank too much, which was pretty regularly, I turned into a puddle of tears.

I figured that this darkness was just part of my personality. My wardrobe was mostly black long before I moved to New York City. I read depressing poetry as if I were a member of the *Dead Poets Society*. My playlists were filled with sad breakup ballads whether I was going through one or not. A doodled stick figure of me jumping out of the skyscraper where I worked appeared regularly in the margins of my notepad.

I never thought I was depressed because I've always had legitimate reasons to feel sad. My mom has had multiple sclerosis since I was a child, and it always seems to be getting worse. My dad died of a heart attack when I was twenty-one. Then, there are the things we have all dealt with: Terrorism. Hurricanes. Mass shootings. Breakups. Fear of failure. Between my own dramas and the crappy state of the world, I was perpetually on the verge of sobbing.

Enter my little brother, Jay. During his senior year of high school, he totaled his car driving under the influence, was dumped by his girlfriend, and didn't seem to have much in common with his friends except for smoking pot, which he did a lot. (See, totaling car.) His grades were on a steady decline and getting into a good college was no longer an option.

Even though we were nine years apart, Jay and I had always been super close. So, while I was no pro at the adulting thing, I thought I could help him get his shit together. After he finished high school, I invited him to crash at my place for six weeks so he could look for a job and an apartment, and take a few college classes.

But, instead of getting serious about school, Jay became obsessed with 9/11 conspiracy theories. He believed that an evil group of people he called "The Cahoots" were behind the attacks. The Cahoots were videotaping his every move and broadcasting it on TV 24/7. They were responsible for draining his bank account and keeping him awake at night. Whenever he did close his eyes, they'd crawl into his mind and tamper with his dreams. Some days, they put a drug in his food that sped up time.

The most disturbing thing was that whenever Jay talked about the Cahoots, he was terrified. Not only were they real to him, they were also threatening his life.

It took a while for me to piece together what was happening to my brother, but after some intense Googling and talking with a psychologist, I learned that Jay was experiencing classic symptoms of schizophrenia. The first wave of symptoms is known as *negative* because they take away something you once had. They include making bad decisions, not caring about your life, barely talking, and being unable to stick to a plan. The *positive* symptoms—which are not at all positive—are things a healthy person wouldn't typically experience unless he or she was tripping. They include hearing voices and seeing people and objects that aren't there. But the hallmark positive symptom is the paranoid belief that people are reading your thoughts, plotting against you, or trying to kill you.

Jay was over eighteen, which meant that even though he was completely out of it, legally he had to be the one to decide if he wanted to see a doctor. I couldn't force him to do it. Finally, after six months of my relentless begging, he checked himself into a mental hospital. He signed an agreement granting me one-time-only access to his medical records, and that's when a psychiatrist informed me he had almost all of the positive and negative symptoms of schizophrenia. She prescribed Invega, an antipsychotic medication that would dull his symptoms. He stayed in the hospital for a week, but never took a single pill. Like many people with schizophrenia, he didn't believe that he was sick. He thought the medication was all a part of the Cahoots' plan.

A little more than a year after his high school graduation, Jay left his keys on the coffee table of his apartment and walked out onto the streets. In the days that followed, I spent hours on the phone with detectives, social workers, and even the FBI, frantically trying to track him down. I counted each day he was missing until the days became weeks—until the number was so high that I wondered if he was even still alive.

That number was about the only thing I continued to keep track of. Dirty clothes and dishes piled up at home and dead-lines were missed at work. I cried often, but especially during thunderstorms, a reminder that wherever my brother was, he was unprotected. My boss offered to let me take some time off from work, but I wanted to be there, even if I was just a waste of space. I wanted to be *fine*. I SAID I WAS FINE, OK? I marked off the hours as they passed like a prisoner in a jail cell. Each little line on a Post-it represented an hour that I'd spent in public, engaged in life, when all I wanted to do was lay in bed.

My bed was the place I could go to check out of reality. I spent hours lying awake, letting my mind drift into darkness. I thought about what it would be like to disappear from the world. If I were gone, the pain would be over—at least for me. I thought about how I might end my life, and who would even care. In my worst moments, I couldn't think of any reasons to stay alive, except that I didn't want to abandon my brother, wherever he was.

I was very angry with everyone in my life for not understanding how much or why I was hurting, and I showed it—so much so that it took true bravery for my aunt to suggest that I consider taking an antidepressant. I had always worried that taking medication would dampen my creativity and weaken my writing by making me numb to my emotions. But at that point, I realized, being numb would be an improvement. So, I allowed myself to do what my brother wouldn't: I saw a psychiatrist who diagnosed me with major depression and (bonus!) generalized anxiety disorder. It was not a pleasant experience, but deep down I knew that I couldn't keep up the charade that I was FINE much longer. Nervously, I began to swallow twenty milligrams of Lexapro every day.

During the first couple of days, I felt sort of giddy, high, then incredibly tired; but within a few weeks, I realized that the meds were having a positive effect. It became harder for me think about all of the terrible things that might be happening to Jay. It was as if the Lexapro had built a wall to block out the negative thoughts. I could still climb over it, back into my dark place—and sometimes I did—but I began to spend more and more time thinking about what I *could* do, which was to start taking care of myself again.

Therapy, with which I had had an on-and-off relationship since my parents' divorce when I started elementary school, became about dealing with my symptoms instead of talking about everyone else. I started going to the gym before work and joined a rec soccer team, so I'd have something to do every weekend.

I was so wrong about how taking an antidepressant would affect my writing. For one thing, it's hard to do *anything* when you are as depressed as I was, let alone something creative. Depression makes you very, very tired. If I did lose any of my powers on Lexapro—which I doubt—I gained the ability to focus on my work, rather than expending all my energy obsessing over everything that was wrong with my life and the world.

I started writing essays about what was happening with my brother, who had resurfaced but was committed to living on the street. In response to my pieces, more than a hundred people e-mailed or messaged to tell me that they were going through the same thing with their brother/sister/daughter/son/friend/etc. Many of them asked for advice, but I didn't have any. All I could think was, "I am not alone in this—so why aren't more people talking about it?"

Jay stayed on the streets. He hitchhiked through twenty-seven states, panhandling, and talking to (or yelling at) anyone who would listen about the Cahoots and his other delusions. I saw him a few times when he circled back to New York or camped out for a few weeks with our mom in Texas.

The constant movement from town to town gave him something to fill his days other than watching cable news hoping to catch a story about the Cahoots. But living on the street is dangerous, and I knew it. Although I wasn't crying about it all the time anymore, I constantly worried that something terrible would happen to him. And ultimately, it did.

Three years into this nightmare, at only twenty-one, my little brother killed himself. I was devastated. Losing a sibling so early in the game is one of the things that you can't prepare for or recover from. Part of you stays broken.

There is a constant debate among psychiatrists about the amount of time someone can grieve before it turns into an episode of depression. I was determined not to let that happen. I immediately upped my therapy sessions to twice a week and worked through the messy stages of grief. I accepted that my brother's short life ended in a tragedy. I realized that I didn't only lose my brother; I lost years of my own life because I didn't know it was possible to feel better. I didn't know that there was a way to keep the darkness from taking over my mind.

Becoming a Do-Gooder

I randomly applied for a job at the National Suicide Prevention Lifeline, the government-funded crisis hotline contacted by more than a million people each year. Having worked exclusively for magazines, I didn't know the first thing about nonprofit communications. Looking back now, it was a radical thing to do. It was too soon after Jay's death to make such a massive career change. But as it turned out, diving straight into a career that felt meaningful to me ended up being one of best things I have ever done.

Once I was on the inside, I learned that psychologists and social workers have basically invented another language to talk about mental health. There were so many words and acronyms I didn't know—starting with my own label: SOSL (Survivor of Suicide Loss.) I did know that people were desperate for help and shouldn't have to learn a foreign language to get it, so I became an advocate of "real talk," encouraging people on the inside to use language that real people (not clinicians) could understand.

After three years at the Lifeline, I moved on to Fountain House, a nonprofit that helps people with bipolar disorder and schizophrenia find jobs, get housing, and live a better life. Until I went to Fountain House, my brother was the only person with schizophrenia I had ever actually met. There, I got to know hundreds of people who showed up every day to help one another live a better life and work toward educational and career goals. You'll meet some of them in this book. Today, I work at Phoenix House, a national nonprofit addiction treatment center. Since drug overdoses are at an all-time high, it's more important than ever to engage in real talk about treatment and recovery.

As I gathered experience in my new field, I learned that the reason half of all people with mental illness don't receive treatment has little to do with science or medicine. Medications and therapies, while imperfect, exist, but public policy and the complexity of the health care system make getting treatment a battle in itself. I figured that if I could learn how health policy is made, it would help me connect people to the right treatment. So, I went to grad school. After four looooong years of working during the day, going to classes at night, and studying on the weekend, I earned a Masters in Public Health.

A couple of years into my new career, I met my now-husband, Barry. I would vomit if I had to read how happy we are together, so I'll spare you that. What's important is that there is no possible way I would have met Barry if I hadn't gotten treatment for my depression—and not just because I was barely getting out of bed. I was hurting so much that I couldn't give or receive love. I hated myself. It's not a great look, and it doesn't lead to finding your person.

BUT ENOUGH ABOUT ME...

Let's talk about you. You may be hurting right now, but I want you to take a deep breath and commit to reading this book. It's the first step to getting to OK. You may not have a clue how to deal with your mental health right now, and it might get a little worse before it gets OK, but it will. Everything really is going to be OK because you are no longer in the dark about your health and emotions. Actually, it will get a lot *better* than OK. You can have the awesome life you've always wanted.

PART ONE

Choose Your Own Adventure

Life is an adventure. If you are among the one-in-five people with a mental disorder, yours is going to be a little more action-packed. You don't get to choose which mental disorder you have (or most of the things life throws your way), but you *do* get to decide how you will handle it. Learning about your illness puts you in the driver's seat and empowers you to map out a plan to recovery.

This part of the book explains what it feels like to have certain mental illnesses. It isn't meant to help you diagnose yourself. (Neither is the internet, BTW.) But it will help you understand more about the symptoms you are experiencing. If you haven't been given a diagnosis but recognize some of these symptoms, bookmark the page and show it to your doctor or therapist. You may notice that your symptoms match a couple of disorders. That's because many of them go together like PB&J.

Along with information on each mental disorder, there is a story about someone who has struggled with it and found their way to a good place, albeit with some bumps along the way. They have shared their adventures to help you feel less alone and inspire you to keep going. You might recognize what they are going through, but since mental illness manifests differently in everyone, you might not. Again, it's not your job to diagnosis yourself.

Before we get started, this is the golden rule: If you want to die, you need to get help ASAP. There are so many people who want you to stay here with us. You can talk, text, or chat with someone right this second if you need to. Their contact info is waiting for you in part ten whenever you need it.

Words Matter

I want to be clear about two words I often use—*diagnosis* and *symptoms*. No matter what disorder you have, you are a person with [insert diagnosis here] who is experiencing [insert symptom here]. You are not your diagnosis or your symptoms. You are not bipolar. You are not manic. Although some of these disorders are chronic, meaning you may experience them off and on for a lifetime, you will always be *you*, who also happens to have a mental disorder—just as someone might have diabetes. While we're on the topic, *mental illness* and *mental disorder* mean the same thing and are interchangeable.

Just as you wouldn't presume to tell someone he has diabetes unless you've had some legit medical training, you shouldn't go around diagnosing people with a mental disorder. If you are reading this book because you care about someone who may have an issue, it can be tempting to tell her exactly how she should handle it. Try to remember that she is on her own adventure. There is a thin line between helping someone and acting like a jerk. Trust me, I've been a jerk.

THE "BIBLE" OF PSYCHIATRY

Mental illness is defined, more or less, by the American Psychiatric Association (known as APA). It's a group of psychiatrists, best known for publishing *The Diagnostic and Statistical Manual of Mental Diagnosis*. The *DSM* is considered the bible by mental health pros because it lists the criteria for diagnosing a variety of mental illnesses. Unlike most physical illnesses, mental disorders cannot be identified with the help of lab tests and exams. Psychiatrists have to make decisions based largely on their own evaluations and judgment. As culture changes, so has the *DSM*.

Over the past sixty-five years, five different editions and two significant revisions have been published with its authors making massive updates along the way. The most recent version, the *DSM-5*, would make Bill Nye the Science Guy proud because the APA spent more than a decade reviewing clinical research to make sure that each diagnosis was supported by science. Which is nice, since it's still the guide that doctors, insurance companies, government agencies, drug companies, and the justice system use to determine who has a mental disorder.

But I don't suggest you drop everything and order a copy from Amazon. For starters, it's 970 pages. Even if you feel up to reading it, you may believe you have a dozen different disorders after reading the individual symptoms for each illness. It really takes a mental health pro to figure our which symptoms are clinically significant.

IF FREUD COULD TEXT

These emojis, which I use throughout the book, explain what treatment works best for each disorder according to stacks of research, recommendations from the National Institute of Mental Health, and the advice of a few psychiatrists I consider to be rock stars. You'll find more details about treatment options in part two.

= Cognitive Behavioral Therapy (CBT)

= Dialectical Behavior Therapy (DBT)

= Electroconvulsive Therapy (ECT)

= Exposure Therapy

= Eye-Movement Desensitization and Reprocessing (EMDR)

= Family Therapy

= Hospitalization

= Light Therapy

= Medication

= Medical Care

= Nutrition Counseling

= Psychotherapy

= Group Therapy

= Transcranial Magnetic Stimulation (TMS)

MAJOR DEPRESSION

AKA: Clinical depression, major depressive disorder, depression

How it feels: A wave of nothingness washes over you and knocks you on your ass. You can't even...with anyone or anything. You stop going out. You stop talking to people unless you absolutely have to. You don't care anymore. You are nothing. Nothing matters.

What it is: There's a big difference between feeling bummed or having a down day and experiencing major depression. For one thing, depression isn't just a feeling; it's an illness that can make you feel incredibly sad, hopeless, and angry. It can make your body ache with heartburn, muscle pain, headaches, and stomach trouble. Sometimes people with depression don't even feel sad—just angry or dead inside.

Depression has been around about as long as humans have. Back in the B.C. days, the ancient Greek physician Hippocrates began diagnosing patients with *melancholia* when they were sad and out of it. Since then, a wide variety of treatments has been developed to help you get on top of that wave of nothingness and ride it to shore.

What it is not: Depression is *not* the grief we all feel after losing someone or something. It's not feeling really bummed or coming down hard after a bender.

Symptoms: Depression can be mild, moderate, or severe, based on how many symptoms you have. It's diagnosed when you feel sad or pissed off every day for at least two weeks without an obvious trigger, and includes some or all of these:

- Not wanting to do things you used to love
- Losing or gaining a bunch of weight without trying
- Having trouble sleeping or snoozing way more than usual
- Feeling like you are moving and talking in slo-mo
- Having no energy
- Feeling worthless
- Feeling very guilty
- Having trouble focusing or making even tiny decisions
- Wanting to die and thinking about how to make it happen

Who gets it: Depression is one of the most common mental illnesses. It strikes seven percent of all Americans each year, which is twenty-two million people. Those between the ages of eighteen and twenty-nine are more likely to have it than others, and it is slightly more common in women than men.

How to deal:

Good to know: Depression manifests itself a little differently in men and women. Women often feel sad and excessively guilty, while guys are more likely to be angry and have trouble sleeping.

VIPs who have talked about their experiences with depression:
Alicia Keys, Mandy Moore, Dwayne "The Rock" Johnson, Sarah Silverman, Wayne Brady

Seasonal Affective Disorder

AKA: SAD, winter depression

What it is: Seasonal affective disorder is a subtype of depression that some people get when the seasons change. It's not strictly a winter thing. Most people with SAD start to feel it in late fall, but some experience it in the warmer months. SAD usually isn't as debilitating as major depression, but it can zap your energy and put you in a bad mood. You may feel hopeless, have a hard time concentrating, and stop giving a shit about things you used to love. Just because your SAD symptoms go away when the season changes doesn't mean you should tough it out. We only get so many days in life, and spending a quarter or more of the year in a funk isn't cool.

What it is not: An excuse for not leaving your house in the winter (or any time).

Symptoms of Winter SAD:

- Grouchiness
- Being really tired for no reason
- Feeling easily insulted
- Trouble getting along with other people
- Sleeping more
- Eating way more carbs than usual
- Feeling heaviness in arms and legs (and not just because of extra carbs)
- Weight gain

Symptoms of Summer SAD:

- Feeling sad
- Lots of anxiety
- Trouble sleeping
- Weight loss
- Not being hungry

Who gets it: Depending on where you look, between one (in sunny Florida) and nine (in mostly cold New Hampshire) percent of Americans deal with SAD, and three out of four of them are women. SAD mainly strikes people between the ages of eighteen and thirty and is more common in colder climates.

How to deal:

CARLA JEAN'S ADVENTURE

A few years ago, I regularly found myself on the floor in the bathroom at my office, crying. I wasn't just crying at work. Sometimes I would take a book to a bar and end up crying in public. It made people uncomfortable, but it was better than crying and wallowing at home.

It was February, which was already the worst month for me. My boyfriend had broken up with me, and I was crushed by an intense sense of hopelessness. I didn't think I would ever find anyone again. I kept thinking, "It's all over for me." My friends tried to reassure me, telling me that I wasn't realistic. But when you have a cloud of depression hanging over you, reality is irrelevant.

After about a month of crying and feeling totally hopeless, I went to see a therapist. By the end of the first appointment, she said, "It sounds like you have a history of depression and seasonal affective disorder. Does this sound right to you?" That moment was freeing because she gave me the opportunity to say, "No, you are way off base." By asking if I agreed with her assessment, she helped me be an active participant in my care.

My therapist also asked me if I would be comfortable taking medication. I started taking Zoloft, and within a few weeks, I felt much stronger. I went from feeling that I was made of glass to believing I was solid, and that I could deal with whatever happened. I still experience highs and lows of emotion, but the lows no longer felt like they might destroy me.

"I still experience highs and lows of emotion, but the lows no longer felt like they might destroy me."

I turned to yoga, which I had recently started practicing. I've found it to be a valuable companion to therapy. It helps me get out of my head and allows me to work through a problem on my mat.

For me, seasonal affective disorder is a less intense version of depression. Now I know how to recognize the feeling, and I understand that it will pass. I just grab my light therapy lamp to help it along.

Knowing that I have support from people in my life is vital to staying on top of my mental health. I know it can be challenging to be friends with someone who has depression because many of my friends have said so. Now, I try to be straightforward with people who don't know how to support me when I am struggling. I've learned which people in my life think that therapy is BS, and I don't reach out to them when I need support.

Not everyone is comfortable talking about their mental health, but I feel like I can carry the torch. I've had many friends and colleagues come to me for information about getting therapy, and it's gratifying to be able to help.

I CAN'T TODAY, I'M PLANNING ON WORRYING ABOUT SOMETHING FOR ABOUT THREE HOURS WITHOUT ANY REASON, THEN BEATING MYSELF UP ABOUT WASTED TIME AND ENERGY, THEN GOING ON A LONG, NICE WALK TO RECOVER... MAYBE GET A SNACK.

GENERALIZED ANXIETY DISORDER

AKA: Anxiety

How it feels: Let's say you are applying to grad school. You worked your butt off in college, got a 4.0, and aced the GRE. Even though everyone says you'll be accepted into some of your top-choice programs, you doubt it. Why would they let you in? Getting rejected will be so mortifying. You might as well pull your applications.

What it is: Anxiety is probably the most common—and misunderstood—of all mental disorders. For one thing, most people feel anxious about things: first dates, big tests, speaking in public. But feeling anxious about something is not the same as having an anxiety disorder. An anxiety disorder is when you can't focus on your life because you are so worried about all of the "what ifs." It's about having a reaction that is out of proportion with the situation. It's the difference between being nervous about going on a job interview and feeling that getting the job is a life-or-death situation. Fear is at the heart of anxiety. It triggers a "fight or flight" response in your body, making your heart race, hands sweat, and breath come faster. Anxiety is when someone expects to be in danger but really isn't.

What it is not: Anxiety is not worry, fear of something legitimately dangerous or scary, stress, nervousness, or "butterflies."

Symptoms:

- Feeling anxious or worried about various things throughout most of the day, for six months or longer
- Not being able to stop thinking about the things that worry you, even when you try
- Being restless
- Feeling as if you are moving and talking in slo-mo
- Having trouble sleeping
- Getting pissed off easily
- Having tight muscles (not from hitting the gym)

Who gets it: About three percent of Americans experience anxiety each year. That's around ten million people. It's typically diagnosed at around age thirty, and women are twice as likely to have it.

How to deal: 🗨 🔍 💊 🛋 👭

Good to know: Anxiety and depression are a power couple. Often, insomnia is the third wheel.

VIPs who have talked about their experiences with anxiety: Author John Green, Kristen Bell, Kristen Stewart, Rachel Bloom

Social Anxiety Disorder

AKA: Social phobia

What it is: There's a difference between feeling nervous about meeting someone new and being so afraid that the new person won't like you that you decide to stay at home and turn off your phone. Social anxiety disorder is a subtype of anxiety that refers explicitly to an intense fear of social interactions. It can make everyday life so hard that you tend not to go out, stick to just a few friends, and choose jobs where you won't have to talk to many people.

What it is not: Being a loner or an introvert, who needs alone time to recharge

Symptoms:

- Extreme anxiety about being in a place where people may watch or judge you
- Fear that you will do something to make people dislike or reject you
- Sweating or shaking in anticipation of being in a social setting
- Almost always feeling anxious about being out in public
- Avoiding people, places, and activities because of anxiety

Who gets it: Social anxiety is even more common than generalized anxiety disorder. About seven percent of Americans, aka twenty-two million people, have it, and it usually shows up in between the ages of eight and fifteen.

How to deal: 💭 🔍 👭

VIPs who have talked about their experiences with social anxiety: Britney Spears, Jennifer Lawrence, Ricky Williams

RENÉE'S ADVENTURE

Anxiety has been a part of my life since I was a kid. Back in elementary school, I would get so nervous about leaving my classroom to go to another class that I would start shaking. I started therapy for anxiety and PTSD after I was injured in a car accident as a teen. But those experiences were nothing compared to the totally debilitating anxiety I would feel after my dad died.

My dad was the parent who raised me, and losing him was a big defining moment in my life. At the time, I was going to college and working in Denver. I spent a few weeks after his death in Ohio, not wanting to go home. My dad was my safety net, and without him, I wasn't sure how I could return to my life.

Once I made it back to Colorado, I refused to leave the house. I was terrified of sunlight or any light touching me. I started locking myself in the bathroom so I could sit in the dark all day. I couldn't eat. I didn't want to watch TV. I just wanted to be alone, in the dark.

My aunt told me that even though I was grieving, it wasn't "normal" to starve myself and hide out in the bathroom. Part of me must have agreed because I let her take me to the student health center on campus. Luckily there was a psychiatrist on duty. She diagnosed me with generalized anxiety disorder and prescribed Zoloft.

Once I started taking Zoloft, I felt like big waves were constantly washing over me. After about three weeks of vomiting every day, my psychiatrist switched my medication to Paxil. It just made the anxiety worse. I was as wired as if I'd had five cups of coffee. Then we tried Wellbutrin, which turned me into a rage monster. The medication trials continued until we finally found something that worked for me: Prozac.

Prozac diffused my anxiety and made me a lot calmer. I was able to think more clearly which allowed me to recognize my anxious thoughts. On Prozac, I was finally able to function—to go back to school and work, and start living my life.

The right medication and therapy have helped, but I rely on my coping skills to get through each day. Even if it's only a few minutes, I make time for self-care. For me, that means meditating in the sun (I like it now!) or practicing deep breathing. Sometimes I know why I am anxious, but other times I don't. Journaling usually helps me get to the bottom of it. None of these techniques work 100% the time. If you have generalized anxiety disorder, there might be a background level of anxiety that is always present, like a refrigerator humming.

"If you have generalized anxiety disorder, there's a background level of anxiety that is always present, like a refrigerator humming."

Anxiety is a real illness, and it manifests differently in everyone. Public speaking is one aspect of my career, and I feel completely comfortable standing up in front of a thousand people. But if I'm in a social setting with just five people, I might be a nervous wreck. The key is to learn how to reduce my anxiety, soothe myself, and reset.

My cats, Pierre and Gracie, are also a tremendous comfort. When I feel my anxiety levels rising, I take a kitty break to play or snuggle with my cats. Sometimes, just looking at them while they're napping helps me calm down. There are days when I feel like I can't "people." My cats don't judge me. They don't care what I'm wearing or if I brushed my hair or my teeth that day. They just love me.

PANIC DISORDER

AKA: Panic attacks

What it feels like: Your heart is racing, hands sweating, and you can't breathe. You may you feel like you are choking, that you might faint—or even that you are having a heart attack.

What it is: "OMG, I'm having a panic attack" might be something your overly dramatic friend says when she can't find her keys—but that isn't exactly accurate. A panic attack is not the next level of freaking out; it's an actual physical reaction to fear, and it can be scary as hell. Seriously...it can feel like a heart attack, complete with heart palpitations, chest pain, shaking, sweating, and difficulty breathing.

If you have panic attacks often—from a few times a week to a few times a month—you are probably experiencing panic disorder. One of the weird things about panic attacks is that they seem to come out of nowhere. There's usually no real danger or obvious reason for them.

What it is not: A heart attack

Symptoms: During a panic attack, you feel at least four of these things:

- Heart pounding
- Sweating
- Shaking
- Can't breathe
- Feeling of choking

- Chest pain
- Nausea
- Chills
- Numbness
- Dizziness
- Sudden fear of dying
- Feeling that you're losing your mind

Who gets it: About three percent of people in the US, that's ten million, have panic disorders. As with anxiety, women are twice as likely to be diagnosed. People with panic disorder may start having panic attacks in their teens or early twenties.

How to deal: 💭 🔍 💊 🛋 👫

Good to know: Many people feel as if they are dying when they have their first panic attack, and often head to the ER. The attacks usually last about ten minutes but can go on for an hour. Other than calming you down and making sure that you aren't having a heart attack, there's not much the ER docs can do for you. A panic attack doesn't do any major damage to your body—which doesn't mean it's NBD, because, recap: You feel like you are dying.

VIPs who have talked about their experiences with panic attacks: Amanda Seyfried, Ellie Goulding, Emma Stone, John Mayer, Lena Dunham

HEATHER'S ADVENTURE

My first panic attack came on when I was eleven. My chest tightened up, and my throat felt like it was closing. My heart beat very fast. I felt like the world was ending and that I was going to die. It was so intense and overwhelming that I thought I was having a heart attack.

I told my parents that I felt like I couldn't breathe. I had already been diagnosed with anxiety, so they said it was probably part of that. That reassured me, but the physical symptoms were scary. I wondered if I would have to deal with symptoms like these for the rest of my life.

After going through a rough period of depression, anxiety, and suicidal thoughts when I was a freshman in high school, I felt like no one cared about me. I stopped hanging out with my friends and spent more and more time alone.

I began to cut myself and soon I couldn't stop. I started to think about killing myself. When these thoughts became unbearable, and I truly considered acting on them, I decided to call the National Suicide Prevention Lifeline. The counselor connected me to my therapist, who got in contact with my family. They decided it was best to take me to a psychiatric hospital.

"I spent a lot of time with other teens in the hospital. Listening to their stories inspired me to keep living."

At the hospital, I learned some new coping skills. We did an activity where we drew our "go-to" ways of coping, and I was able to think of music and even something as simple as doing my makeup to get my mind off of things. That worked for me. I spent a lot of time with other teens there and made some friends. Listening to the other patients' stories inspired me to keep living.

While I was in the hospital, I started taking Prozac. It worked well for a while, but I ended up having to get off of it because it made me gain a lot of weight. I now take Zoloft and Vyvanse, and the combo has worked for me ever since. I began seeing a therapist who practiced cognitive behavioral therapy (CBT). She helped me learn to focus on identifying unhealthy or unhelpful thoughts and replacing them with more productive ones.

I tend to isolate myself when I have a panic attack. I know it is better to talk to someone supportive about how I'm feeling, but I still find it hard to explain to my friends what is going on. I want to hide. I find myself apologizing over and over and wishing that I could be normal.

Panic attacks aren't always obvious. They don't always include crying and hyperventilating or that "heart attack" sensation. But even if they aren't dramatic, they should be taken seriously.

OBSESSIVE-COMPULSIVE DISORDER

AKA: OCD

How it feels: You are obsessed with a belief, such as, you have to wash your hands six times for one minute each time, or you will get sick and maybe die.

What it is: You may think OCD applies to anyone who is uptight or particular about something—like lining up his books in alphabetical order or insisting on running five miles each morning—but it's a real disorder that makes people miserable. OCD can make you obsess over a certain idea or have an irresistible urge to perform a ritual (such as checking the door eight times to make sure it's locked) to the point that it interrupts your daily life.

Everyone obsesses about things from time to time, but an OCD-level obsession is when you can't stop thinking about something that you would rather not think about, so much that it gets in the way of everything else. A compulsion is something you feel like you *have to do* to prevent something terrible from happening, such as checking the stove ten times to make sure it is off.

What it is not: Simply being a perfectionist, getting hyper-focused on formatting a Google Doc, washing the dishes ASAP after every meal

Symptoms: Someone with OCD has at least one obsession or compulsion that takes more than an hour a day to deal with and gets in the way of his life. Some common obsessions and rituals are:

- Excessively hand washing due to fear of germs or contamination
- Constantly texting and calling friends or family because you're worried they will be hurt
- Repeatedly counting things because you are afraid of losing something
- Arranging and rearranging objects until they are in symmetrical or "perfect" order

Who gets it: About one percent of Americans have OCD, adding up to three million people. It can start in childhood, but most people are diagnosed in their late teens and twenties.

How to deal: 💬 🔍 💊 🛋️

VIPs who have talked about their experiences with OCD: Billy Bob Thornton, Charlize Theron, David Beckham, Jessica Alba

TRISH'S ADVENTURE

It started with my bedroom doorknob. When I was eight years old, I began standing outside of my room every night, sometimes for fifteen minutes, turning the knob to the left and right, over and over before I felt it was OK to go in.

I would wash my hands until they were red and raw, concerned that I couldn't get them clean enough. Using a public restroom was a traumatic experience. Each time I'd have to really examine the toilet stall and seat, and after I deemed it acceptable,

I would only squat. I knew the facts, but I was convinced that I would get AIDS, herpes, or HPV from the toilet seat—or even wind up pregnant.

Once I started driving, I was afraid that I would hit someone with my car and not realize it. I'd actually turn the car around to go back and check that I hadn't run over anyone, which made me late a lot of the time.

For the most part, I kept these, along with dozens of obsessions and compulsions to myself. It was hard for me to describe what was going on without sounding psychotic, which wasn't the case. It was a feeling I had—not a hallucination. The shame and fear of embarrassing myself were stronger than any of my anxieties.

No one knew what was happening inside my mind. From the outside, my life looked great. I did well in school, had friends, and a boyfriend, and at twenty-five, I was well on my way to earning a PhD in English literature.

It wasn't until a very stressful period, while studying for my doctoral exam, that my anxiety became so intense, I had to reach out. I hadn't slept more than a few hours a night for two weeks. I was having panic attacks that made me feel like I was going to die, and at the time, I actually wanted to die. I asked my boyfriend to take me to the hospital.

After a week in the hospital, mostly spent trying to sleep, I got connected to a therapist who I really clicked with. I was in acute distress from anxiety those first few months, but after awhile we were able to dig into my, until now, undiagnosed OCD. We began cognitive behavioral therapy (CBT) and exposure therapy, which helped me come up with strategies to defeat my obsessions and compulsions. For example, I would repeat affirmations to myself like "there is nothing on this seat" or "this food is not poisonous."

I also saw a psychiatrist. Unlike a lot of people, I was always OK with the idea of taking psychiatric medication. I remembered reading Prozac Nation, and wondering if there was a pill that would quiet the cycle of anxious and obsessive thoughts that created a storm in my mind. I began taking an SSRI, first Zoloft and then Lexapro, along with Klonopin. It took a little while to get it right, but eventually, medication empowered me to think more rationally.

People call OCD the "doubting disease" because you never really know what's going on. Sometimes these anxieties are based in reality. It can be hard to make the distinction between what is OCD and what is common sense— especially when it comes to avoiding germs or staying safe.

> **"It can be hard to make the distinction between what is OCD and what is common sense."**

Dealing with my disorder takes a lot of work. I have to be sure that I am getting enough sleep and surround myself with people who help me practice coping strategies. Often, I just have to push through no matter how uncomfortable I am.

POST-TRAUMATIC STRESS DISORDER

AKA: PTSD

How it feels: Every time you close your eyes, you relive the worst moment of your life.

What it is: This one pretty much means what it says. PTSD is stress that comes on as a result of experiencing something traumatic. Usually, the trauma is something horrible you've lived through or seen IRL. People tend to use the term about veterans, but you don't have to have been on the front lines of a war to have PTSD. The trauma might be something like living through a natural disaster or watching someone die in a car accident. While seeing a terrorist attack on TV is traumatic, it is unlikely to create that same "fight or flight" response in your body. That's why the *DSM* defines *trauma* as something that could have caused injury or death.

Obviously, if you have been assaulted or seen someone die you're going to have a lot of feelings about it. It's not something you can just shake off. You'll probably feel really sad, angry, guilty, scared, or ashamed—but that doesn't mean you have PTSD. Most people who experience these things bounce back pretty quickly. It is those who still feel traumatized months or even years later who are diagnosed with PTSD, which involves experiencing that feeling of trauma again and again in nightmares, sudden memories, and flashbacks.

What it is not: Being weak

Symptoms: If you have gone through something that could have caused injury or death to you or someone in your presence, you have experienced the *DSM* definition of *trauma*. You may suffer from PTSD if you exhibit one or more of these symptoms a month or more after the trauma:

- Memories of the trauma that suddenly pop up in your mind
- Nightmares about of the trauma or the way you felt during it
- Flashbacks that make you act or feel as if it is happening again
- Major stress when you see or hear things that remind you of the trauma
- Rapid heartbeat, dizziness, or sweating when you think about the trauma
- Going out of your way to avoid people, places, or things that remind you of the trauma
- Trying hard not to think about the trauma because of how it will make you feel

Or if you have two or more of these symptoms:

- Being unable to remember what happened (assuming you didn't hurt your head or blackout during the trauma)
- Feeling as if you are bad, cursed, dirty, or other negative things you didn't think about yourself before
- Being angry, scared, or ashamed a lot of the time
- Being unable to feel happy or loved
- Feeling distant from other people

- Not being interested in doing things you normally like to do, even if they have nothing to do with the trauma
- Blaming yourself for what happened when it clearly wasn't your fault
- Having angry outbursts
- Acting reckless and self-destructive
- Being on high alert for danger
- Having trouble staying focused
- Being really scared by sudden noises such as a car alarms
- Having trouble falling asleep or staying awake

Who gets it: It's hard to pin down the number of people who have PTSD, partly because it's a new-ish name for something people have been experiencing for a long time. About thirty percent of people who have been sexually abused have some PTSD symptoms, and about fifteen percent of all vets from Iraq and Afghanistan have been diagnosed with it.

How to deal:

Good to know: It's common for people with PTSD to have depression, anxiety, and substance use disorder.

VIPs who have talked about their experiences with PTSD: Gabrielle Union, Lady Gaga, Shia LaBeouf, Whoopi Goldberg

BLAKE'S ADVENTURE

Imagine the worst thing that ever happened to you—then imagine it is always playing in your head. It may not be in the front of your mind, but it's always there. That nightmare became my reality during my last semester of college after I found my mother when she hung herself.

About a month after my mother's suicide, my therapist suggested that I might have PTSD. I was NOT happy with that diagnosis. From what I had learned in my psych classes, PTSD was for veterans who had been to war and back. I read about how painful it was for them and couldn't imagine ever having those types of feelings. As far as I could tell, I was grieving.

I thought that by getting myself and my father into treatment immediately, we could avoid PTSD. I couldn't see it, but the symptoms were already in full bloom by the time I went to therapy. I couldn't sleep the night I found my mother, and that turned into insomnia. Some nights I got four hours of sleep, sometimes less. I don't think I ever slept more than five hours a night for a year unless it was one of the rare times when I fell into a coma-like sleep for sixteen hours. When I did sleep, I often had a recurring nightmare that I was finding my mom all over again. Sometimes in my dreams, I was able to stop her. Then I'd wake up and realize that no, she was gone.

I started avoiding things and hiding from life because I never knew how I'd react to triggers. The trauma I'd experienced bled into every part of my life. Sleep deprivation made me hallucinate. One day, not long after my mother died, I went to the science lab on campus and hallucinated a bunch of bodies hanging from the ceiling. I had a panic attack and ran straight to the car. Sometimes I would drive by a friend's house and think I saw someone hanging. I would circle the block until I

"I was being haunted by my mind, obsessing over every detail of what I'd lived through and wishing it were different."

could be sure the body wasn't there. It's like I was being haunted by my mind, obsessing over every detail of what I'd lived through and wishing it were different; hoping there was a clock to turn back or a genie to grant my wish to be normal again—to go back to the way it was before everything changed.

I began eye movement desensitization and reprocessing (EMDR) therapy, which helps you process memories from traumatic experiences. I also learned the difference between "big T" vs. "little t" trauma. I had both. The "big T" was the moment I found my mother. But I had experienced "little t" trauma when I was four years old and my parents often left me alone while they went out to get high.

For a long time after my mother's death, my life revolved around PTSD. Lately, I've been able to focus on my own life. I recently got married and am expecting my first child soon. Growing up, I had always assumed my mother would be here for my university graduation, wedding, and having kids, but that isn't what happened. Life right now is probably the best it has ever been since I lost my mom. I just needed a little help seeing my problem and dealing with it.

REAL TALK:

Only 37% of people surveyed feel as if they know everything they need to know about their mental illness.

BIPOLAR DISORDER

AKA: Manic depressive disorder

How it feels: You accidentally got on a roller coaster ride. Out of nowhere, you are flying high, feeling on top of the world, and then—whoosh—you're at the bottom, sad and hopeless.

What it is: Bipolar disorder causes major shifts in mood and energy. It creates those high highs (mania) and low lows (depression). There are a few different types of bipolar disorder: bipolar I, bipolar II, and cyclothymic disorder. Bipolar I is when you cycle through episodes of mania and depression that interrupt your regular, everyday flow of emotion. Bipolar II isn't a sequel; it means that you experience long episodes of depression and shorter, less intense manic episodes that last only a few days. If you have cyclothymic disorder, you have some but not all of the symptoms of bipolar II.

What it is not: Mood swings, borderline personality disorder

Symptoms: Bipolar disorder is usually diagnosed when someone has an episode of depression or a mild form of mania called hypomania followed by an episode of mania. Symptoms of depression include:

- Feeling sad or pissed off every day for at least two weeks without an obvious trigger
- Not wanting to do things you used to love
- Losing or gaining a bunch of weight without trying
- Having trouble sleeping or sleeping much more than usual

- Feeling like you are moving and talking in slo-mo
- Having no energy
- Feeling worthless
- Having a lot of guilt for no real reason
- Having trouble focusing or making even tiny decisions
- Wanting to die and thinking about how to make it happen

Symptoms of mania include:

Having a burst of energy and elevated mood for several days, plus at least three of the following:

- Extra, extra self-esteem that is unrealistic
- Barely needing sleep
- Being much more talkative than usual
- Having tons of "brilliant" ideas all at once
- Being easily distracted
- Wanting to accomplish major goals—such as making a lot of money or sleeping with a lot of different people—really quickly
- Feeling agitated, pacing around a room or hand-wringing
- Burning through a lot of cash, whether by gambling, shopping, or making quickie investments

Who gets it: More than two percent of all adults in the US— about eight million people—have bipolar disorder. It tends to hit in the mid-twenties, often preceded by a diagnosis of depression before the onset of a manic episode.

How to deal: 🗨 ◎ ⚡ 🏢 🖊 🛋 💀

Good to know: Rapid cycling doesn't mean crushing it in spin class. It is when you've had more than four episodes of mania, hypomania, or depression within one year.

VIPs who have talked about their experiences with bipolar disorder: Catherine Zeta-Jones, Carrie Fisher, Demi Lovato, Mariah Carey

JASON'S ADVENTURE

When I was a kid, happiness seemed so elusive. I could see that plenty of other people were happy and finding joy in life— but I didn't know how to experience it for myself. I was serious and morose, always thinking about what terrible thing might happen next. Especially at night when I'd lay in awake in bed for hours.

I buried myself in my studies, which paid off when I became valedictorian of my high school. In all other ways, I was behind. I didn't have many friends or a girlfriend and never smoked or drank like a lot of my classmates. I wasn't abstaining on purpose, I was just too wrapped up in my negative thoughts to be able to connect with anyone else.

Doing well in high school didn't prepare me for college. I was depressed, but also had so many things I absolutely felt I had to accomplish. One of the things on that list was to lose weight. I decided to run my first-ever 5K, which I trained for by running four or five miles every day. That might have been OK, except that I also restricted my diet to cereal in the morning and fruit at night. I lost almost one hundred pounds until I was down to 119. That was just one of the "all or nothing" behav-

iors that controlled my life.

It didn't take long for me to crash. After my freshman year, I transferred to a college closer to home and moved back in with my parents. I took a psychology class the following year and began diagnosing myself with every mental illness in the textbook. I believed not only that I had every disorder, but that I would end up homeless and alone. For an immature, sub-urban, middle-class white guy, that was the worst thing that could ever happen.

Those obsessive thoughts grew worse over time, and I even-tually quit school. I started drinking with a buddy from work, which worked like a charm to drown out my negative internal monologue. It was part social lubricant, part self-medication. But because once I started drinking, I couldn't stop, it was all very bad for me.

The next few years were a haze of being so depressed I had to be hospitalized, interrupted by reckless stretches of mania. When I was depressed I felt hopeless, doomed to a life of com-plete misery. At one point, I planned to kill my parents and my-self. Instead, I went to therapy appointment I had scheduled and ratted myself out. The therapist insisted that I go back to the hospital. Thank God I did.

After that hospitalization, I started seeing a therapist who di-agnosed me with Bipolar Disorder 2. She introduced me to cognitive behavioral therapy (CBT), which was a godsend. It did not delve into the root causes of my depression, but it was a relief because it gave me an alternative to all of those negative thoughts.

During my manic and depressive periods, I would "psychiatrist shop" in search of pills that made me feel good—but they weren't always the best match for my depression and mania. After years of trial and error, I finally found a combination of medications that work for me: Trazodone, Depakote, Klonopin, and Celexa.

Even though I had been working with an excellent therapist and was on medications, I went through a divorce that triggered a relapse. I had an episode of depression, and then full-blown mania, racking up tons of debt and a quickie marriage (and a quickie divorce).

I didn't have the will to keep fighting for my life. As a last resort, I went to an Alcoholics Anonymous (AA) meeting. It gave me a community and a connection with a higher power. AA provided a spiritual component to my overall recovery that had been the missing piece of the puzzle.

Now I try to manage bipolar disorder the way someone might deal with diabetes. I have to stay vigilant and diligent, making sure that I am getting enough sleep, taking my medication, helping others, and doing spiritual work. If I don't take care of myself, just like someone with a physical illness, there is a pretty good chance that I will wind up in a lot of despair or even dead. Staying in recovery is a lot of work, but it's worth it.

"If I don't take care of myself, just like someone with a physical illness, there is a pretty good chance that I will wind up in a lot of despair or even dead."

EVERYTHING IS GOING TO BE OK

SCHIZOPHRENIA

How it feels: Imagine waking up as the star of a reality TV show, except instead of recording your life for the cameras, the producers and crew are all trying to kill you. It sounds like the plot of a horror film, but it is a common delusion of people who have schizophrenia.

What it is: Schizophrenia disrupts the way you think, see, and hear, making it very hard for you to tell what is real. You might feel as if you have no control over what is happening in your mind or your world. It also includes periods of *psychosis*, where you lose your grip on reality. At these times, it is almost impossible for you to communicate with other people or feel emotions.

The *DSM* describes schizophrenia as a collection of positive, negative, and cognitive symptoms. The positive symptoms are not *positive* as in *good,* but as in something extra you didn't have before. Positive symptoms include delusions, hallucinations, and disorganized thinking. *Delusions* are false beliefs, such as the belief that you are being harassed by the government, or that people are sending you messages through your TV, or that you are God. *Hallucinations* are when you see things that aren't there. *Auditory hallucinations* are voices and sounds that don't exist. Someone with schizophrenia might hear several voices, and they often say terrible things like "Kill yourself"— sometimes in unison. The voices can also talk to each other. Yes, it is creepy. Sometimes schizophrenia scrambles signals in your brain so that your words and actions come out jumbled. That's called *disorganized thinking*.

The *negative* symptoms are things that have been *taken away*. Many negative symptoms are similar to symptoms of depression: feeling tired, wanting to be alone, and not caring about things you used to love. But people with schizophrenia don't feel sad or guilty about not taking part in their own life.

Cognitive symptoms are signs that your mind is not functioning properly. They include being unable to pay attention and having trouble remembering things, even over short periods of time. Another cognitive symptom is a shutdown of *executive functioning*—meaning that you can't solve problems such as planning out your day. Many people with schizophrenia also have *anosognosia*, which is the lack of insight or awareness that you have the illness. Unlike plain old denial, anosognosia prevents you from understanding your condition.

Schizophrenia sounds pretty bad, but there are many things you can do to control the symptoms. Psychiatric drugs can blunt even the most bizarre delusions and hallucinations. The sooner you get treatment; the less severe your schizophrenia will become.

What it is not: Multiple personality disorder

Symptoms: The symptoms of schizophrenia are unusual, so psychiatrists have gotten pretty good at spotting it. But since it is a serious mental illness, they don't want to make a snap diagnosis. Before getting an official diagnosis of schizophrenia, you must experience positive and negative symptoms for at least six months, along with trouble functioning at work or school and issues getting along with people, due to cognitive symptoms. You must also have frequent delusions or hallucinations for at least a month. Your doctor will first want to rule out bipolar disorder and make sure your hallucinations aren't drug-related.

Positive symptoms of schizophrenia include:

- Hearing voices
- Seeing things that aren't there
- Paranoid thoughts
- Saying or writing things that don't make sense

Negative symptoms of schizophrenia include:

- Feeling very tired
- Wanting to be alone
- Having a blank expression
- Not caring about everyday life

Cognitive symptoms of schizophrenia include:

- Being unable to pay attention
- Having trouble remembering things, even for short periods of time
- Having a hard time solving easy problems
- Lacking insight

Who gets it: Schizophrenia is the most common psychotic disorder and about one percent—or three million people in the US—have it. It often comes on gradually, almost always in the late teens and early twenties. Men typically start to show the symptoms a little earlier in their lives than women do.

How to deal: 💭 ⚡ 🏥 💊 🛋 💀

Good to know: It's not hard to imagine why people with schizophrenia would want to drink, smoke pot, or do drugs to help deal. But "self-medicating" when you have schizophrenia is a bad idea because it makes the illness worse and harder to treat. Sometimes those voices tell people to kill themselves, which is part of the reason that one in five people with schizophrenia attempt suicide.

VIPs who have talked about their experiences with schizophrenia: Mathematician John Nash, Fleetwood Mac guitarist Peter Green

Schizoaffective Disorder

How it feels: You hear voices and see things that aren't real, which makes it hard to deal with other people. That's compounded by the fact that you feel very sad and hopeless. Sometimes you get a burst of energy that makes you think you can do anything you want, but it never lasts, and the voices in your head make it impossible for you to know what's real.

What it is: Schizoaffective disorder is a subtype of schizophrenia, combined with either major depression or bipolar disorder. It's a hybrid diagnosis that psychiatrists use when a person is dealing with the delusions and hallucinations of schizophrenia along with the feelings of hopelessness and painful sadness that come with major depression—possibly with episodes of mania. In the beginning, it may seem as if you have just one disorder—either schizophrenia or major depression or bipolar disorder. Unless your doctor really looks at the big picture—at all of your symptoms together—schizoaffective disorder might be misdiagnosed.

Symptoms: The *DSM* says that someone has to meet the criteria for schizophrenia as well as exhibiting symptoms of depression or mania.

Who gets it: Since schizoaffective disorder is so often misdiagnosed, it's hard to know exactly how many people have it. Experts are pretty sure it is less common than schizophrenia and bipolar disorder. Symptoms typically come on between ages sixteen and thirty. Guys tend to get it earlier, but women are slightly more likely to have it.

How to deal: 💭 ⚡ 🏢 💊 🛋 💀

SHANNON'S ADVENTURE

I was living a remarkably normal life in a small town in California with my mom, older sister, and our dogs. I took tap dancing and violin lessons and had good friends at school.

During my senior year of high school, I started to have these graphic nightmares that were realistic and super violent. After a night filled with these horrible dreams, it was tough to get on with my day.

Once, I was standing in front my locker at school, and I saw a grape flying around with wings like it was a bumblebee. I had never done mushrooms or acid, so it was very weird. At first, I thought I was just overtired since those nightmares were messing with my sleep, but the hallucinations kept coming. And, unlike the flying grape, many were like scenes from a horror movie. I saw people hanging from the ceiling by their necks. Once I was taking a shower, and all of the water turned to blood. I also heard voices saying things like, "You are no good. No one likes you. You should crawl into a hole. No one would care."

I told my mom what was happening and went to see a psychiatrist. After about seven months, I was diagnosed with schizophrenia and started taking antipsychotic medication. Initially, I was horrified. I had heard a lot about schizophrenia, and none of it was good. I thought my life was over. I believed I would never get better, that there were no meds that would help me. I wondered if I would spend the rest of my life in a hospital.

At the time, my whole life revolved around school, but I couldn't deal with being there anymore. My high school had a program that let me do my assignments from home, but it sucked. I couldn't see my friends and just felt stuck at home with my hallucinations. I thought people were reading my mind. I couldn't bring myself to trust anyone.

My first year of college was not a great experience. The college environment reminded me so much of high school, where I first started having symptoms. The first semester, I dropped all of my classes except the ones that were fully available online. I signed up for the next semester, thinking I was ready, but withdrew from all my classes again. I was so disappointed in myself.

California held bad memories for me. I needed a change, and the easiest thing was to move in with my dad and stepmom in New York City. I had come to NYC as a kid but had never spent an extensive amount there.

First on my to-do list was to find a psychiatrist. Most of the ones I had seen weren't interested in hearing what I had to say. It was so refreshing to find a psychiatrist who actually wanted to hear my input: what I was willing to try and how the medications made me feel. And, probably because she listened to my opinions, my new psychiatrist was able to help me find the right combo of medication.

> **"Being on the right medication made me feel even better than "normal"—better than I ever thought I would again."**

Since I had lived for seventeen years without symptoms, I knew how it felt to feel good. I wanted that feeling back. Being on the right medication made me feel even better than "normal"— better than I ever thought I would again. It made me feel invincible in a weird sense. Realizing I'd found the right medications was one of the best things I've ever experienced. I also started cognitive behavioral therapy (CBT), which was enormously helpful. CBT gave me tools and strategies to help deal with my symptoms. It was like no other therapy I had ever tried.

Up until that point, I had never known anyone who had successfully conquered any kind of mental health challenge. It made me wonder if I could ever be successful. A Google search led me to Fountain House College Re-Entry, a comprehensive program for people like me, who took time off from school because of a mental illness. In the program, I took cooking classes, yoga, and learned about mindfulness, which has become a big thing for me. They also taught life and academic skills like note-taking. I was able to complete one class, then two, and before I knew it, I was taking a full load of classes.

People think, "You have schizophrenia, and your name is Shannon." They put your disorder before you. There's so much more to me. I am finishing my associate degree in journalism, am in a great relationship with my boyfriend of more than two years, and bake great brownies. Oh—and I have schizophrenia.

BORDERLINE PERSONALITY DISORDER

AKA: BPD

How it feels: It's like you are inside a game of PacMan, just bouncing along, and—BOOM!—someone bumps into you and now you are PISSED. Then, maybe you run into a flashing dot and start going really, really fast, then suddenly you crash again. You are living in a constant emotion storm.

What it is: We all have a collection of traits that make up our personality and determine how we think and act. It seems judgmental to consider these traits *good* or *bad*.

Borderline personality disorder is a misleading, confusing term meant to describe "a pattern of instability in a person's mood, behavior, and self-image." It can cause you to have bursts of depression, anxiety, and anger that last from a few hours to a few days. When you have BPD, emotions are an extreme sport because every feeling is amplified. You aren't bummed, you are in complete despair. You aren't happy, you are bouncing-off-the-wall ecstatic. This leads to a lot of impulsive decisions and makes for all kinds of relationship drama.

You really have to understand the patterns of behavior to know if you are just having a rough time adulting or are actually suffering from BPD. It's tempting to let it all play out, but, as with most mental illnesses, the earlier you get treatment, the better.

What it is not: Bipolar disorder

Symptoms:

- Feeling empty or "dead" inside
- Having no goals, dreams, or values
- Not considering the needs or feelings of other people
- Making frantic efforts to avoid abandonment
- Having "all or nothing" relationships that swing from extreme closeness or love to extreme distance or anger
- Hurting yourself or thinking of suicide frequently
- Engaging in risky behaviors such as spending sprees, unsafe sex, drug use, heavy drinking, reckless driving, or binge eating
- Experiencing bursts of anger, sadness, or anxiety that last from a few hours to days
- Feeling intense anger
- Having stress-related paranoid thoughts
- Feeling cut off from yourself or reality

Who gets it: About three million people have BPD, which makes up one percent of all Americans. It usually starts in the teen years and hits men and women equally hard.

How to deal: 💬 🎯 🏢 🛋️

Good to know: Up to eighty-five percent of people with BPD have another mental disorder as well, often anxiety or addiction.

VIPs who have talked about their experiences with BPD: Brandon Marshall, Pete Davidson

KAT'S ADVENTURE

I used to get really angry about everything. Self-harming was my way of coping with all the anger I had at the world. It started with occasional scratching in middle school. By the time I was sixteen, I was cutting myself with a blade, many times a day, every day. I started losing weight because I was so depressed. I liked how it felt, so I started eating less on purpose until I had a full-blown eating disorder.

My therapist caught me self-harming, and together we told my parents. Eventually, my mom started checking my body for new marks every day. At this point, I had been diagnosed with depression, anxiety, and anorexia; but I thought there had to be something else going on. I started researching borderline personality disorder online and realized it fit me shockingly well.

"When you are young and struggling to figure out what's going on in your life, a diagnosis is something you cling to."

At nineteen, after a long, drawn-out process of testing, I was diagnosed with BPD. My health care professionals had dragged their feet, unwilling to diagnose me with a disorder many incorrectly consider untreatable. Once I got the diagnosis, even though it was scary, it helped me understand myself. When you are young and struggling to figure out what's going on in your life, a diagnosis is something you cling to.

I left school and moved back home so I could be part of full-time dialectic behavioral therapy (DBT) group. DBT is considered the best treatment for BPD. I thought it sounded ridiculous and hokey. They wanted me to do mindfulness, and I was not about it. I realized that I had to try because I had taken this year off. So even though I was a little bit grumpy about it, I decided to open up to the other people in the group. I leaned into DBT, and it changed everything. It saved my life.

Going back to school after my break was hard. Life continues even when you aren't there, and that's hard to deal with. I wanted to distance myself from that terrible first year. When I went back, I joined a dance team and got involved in a mental health awareness group, Active Minds. I still struggled with depression and anxiety and spent a lot of my time at home watching TV. I failed on the social relationship front.

In spring of that year, one of my closet friends from high school killed herself. That was really, really difficult for me. Even though I had gotten better, I believed that suicide was always an option for me. The thought of it was like a safety net. I had never really been on the other side before—reacting to someone else's suicide.

I got through the summer, somehow, still coping with the grief. I was on three medications: a mood stabilizer, an antidepressant, and an antipsychotic. Because of all that, I wasn't able to feel much—but that seemed OK because I didn't know how good I could feel. By fall, I decided I was over-medicated. I quit all of my medications cold turkey, which I would not recommend. It knocked me back into a deep depression. That helped me learn that my baseline is not a healthy place to be. I have to take meds.

My body is littered with scars from my years of cutting. They range from pale white lines that are fading away to raised red marks. It's a bummer. I wish I didn't have them, but I'm at peace with them now.

One of the hallmarks of borderline personality disorder is that we experience intense emotions. Many of us seem to feel everything more strongly than those around us. I like to think of it as being superhuman. In this case, super means to an extreme or excessive degree. The human part comes from the fact that emotions are often considered to be what makes us human. Hence, the term superhuman. We're not better than anyone else; we just have an excess of everything that makes humans human.

EATING DISORDERS

AKA: Anorexia, bulimia, binge-eating disorder

How it feels: You know that dream where you're standing naked in front of an audience? Imagine they are all talking about how fat you are. And every time you eat, you get even fatter.

What it is: Eating disorders disrupt the way you eat—in a bad way. You don't have to be skinny to have an eating disorder. It's not all about weight. People with eating disorders have a distorted body image, meaning they have an unrealistic view of their own body. Eating disorders can do serious damage to your heart and bones, and can even be deadly. There are three main types: anorexia nervosa, bulimia nervosa, and binge-eating disorder.

People with anorexia have an intense fear of gaining weight and limit what they eat. They try hard not to consume many calories and often skip meals or cut out lots of food groups. (Think, "no meat, no dairy, no bread, no sugar.") Their self-esteem is based on how they feel about their body shape and weight.

You probably think bulimia is when someone scarfs down a pizza and then pukes it up, so she doesn't gain the weight. Binge eating and then purging is a typical behavior of bulimia, but the disorder is a bit more complicated. Some people with bulimia try to get rid of the food they eat by excessive exercise or by going on a major fast afterward. A lot of mentally healthy people overdo it with food once in a while—or even pretty often (hello, obesity crisis)—but people with bulimia or binge-eating disorder tend to be regimented about their binges, indulging in this behavior at least once each week. When they binge, they feel out of control, unhappy, and ashamed. The purging that follows is an attempt to regain a sense of well-being. Binge-eating disorder is binging without purging or fasting afterward.

What it is not: A problem only rich white girls deal with

Symptoms: People are typically diagnosed with an eating disorder when they have the following symptoms for at least three months.

Symptoms of anorexia:
- Extreme dieting, especially cutting out entire food groups without a medical reason
- Fear of getting fat, even when you are at a healthy weight or underweight
- Denial that your low weight is a serious problem

Symptoms of bulimia:
- Going on a binge—which means eating a lot of food in a short period of time, maybe a couple of hours. Feeling out of control while you are eating, even if you planned the binge in advance
- Purging the food by throwing up, taking laxatives or diuretics, exercising intensely, or not eating again for a set amount of time

Symptoms of binge-eating disorder:

- Eating massive amounts of food in a short amount time, often in private because you feel embarrassed and ashamed
- Gorging until you feel uncomfortably full or when you weren't even hungry
- Feeling angry or sad after overeating

Who gets it: A whopping thirteen million Americans, aka four percent, deal with an eating disorder at some point in their life. These disorders often pop up as early as the tween years. Although women are more likely to have an eating disorder, "manorexia" is a real thing. Guys make up forty percent of all people with binge-eating disorder.

How to deal: 💭 ⚶ 🏢 💊 ✚ 🍴 🛋 👭

Good to know: Up to twenty percent of people with an eating disorder die if they don't get treatment—more than with any other mental illness.

VIPs who have talked about their experience with eating disorders: Aaron Carter, Gabourey Sidibe, Lily Collins, Zoe Kravitz, Zosia Mamet

ANNIE'S ADVENTURE

I remember watching a film called For the Love of Nancy, *about eating disorders, in my high school health class. It was about a rich blonde girl with anorexia, and I thought, "That will never be me." I'm half Middle Eastern and wouldn't describe*

myself as a "girly girl." I was insecure about my looks, but I certainly wasn't obsessed with looking like a model or movie star.

I had always been on the lower end of a healthy weight, but I gained weight quickly the year before I got my first period. During my junior year of high school, people started to comment on it. My mom always told me I had a big butt, although she meant it to be a good thing. At family gatherings, my weight was always a topic of conversation. Sometimes I was told I was too skinny, other times that I was getting fat or "finally starting to look like a woman."

My relationship with food started to change in my senior year of high school. I was at a healthy weight, but I began measuring my food and counting calories. When I started losing weight, it felt like a huge accomplishment. At the time, I needed to feel like I was making progress toward something. I had always wanted to go to a school out of state, but it wasn't an option for me financially, so I ended up going to a community college in my hometown. I didn't even know what I wanted to study. I felt depressed and hopeless about my future.

The only thing I felt that I could control was my weight. That's when my dieting became extreme. I weighed myself twice a day, but no matter how much I lost, it was never enough. I got down to ninety-three pounds, which, for my five-foot-three frame, is considered dangerously low. I spent the summer after my freshman year with my dad. He was horrified by how thin I had become.

I live in Kentucky, where mental health services are slim. We don't have any inpatient eating disorder centers, and it's hard to find all the resources you need in one place. I first saw a nurse practitioner for my weight a little over a year after I started extreme dieting. I had begun to feel out of control. She referred me to a counselor at the comprehensive health center, where I was able to see a nurse, dietitian, and therapist.

Hearing the therapist say that I had an eating disorder was surreal. Before I found myself struggling I had no clue how eating disorders developed. I thought they were a lifestyle choice, not an illness. But my eating disorder wasn't all about the food. Restricting food is just the way it manifested. I had to change my entire self-perception.

The dietitian gave me a better understanding of how nutrition really works and what a healthy weight is for me. When you starve yourself, you aren't allowing your brain to work properly. Once I began re-feeding myself and got back to a healthy weight, I was able to work on the mental stuff.

The work I had to do to change my self-perception took much longer. I couldn't see reality when I was malnourished. My body image and my outlook on life were extremely distorted, which resulted in daily panic attacks. In therapy, I learned coping skills that helped me deal with my triggers.

Now I make sure to take time every day to take care of myself, which means getting enough sleep and not skipping meals. When things feel overwhelming, I step back and catch my breath instead of beating myself up for feeling bad or tired or upset.

Some people think you choose to have an eating disorder. That couldn't be more wrong. Anybody can suffer from this, not only skinny white girls. Eating disorders do not discriminate by gender, race, ethnicity, or class.

"Eating disorders do not discriminate by gender, race, ethnicity, or class."

SUBSTANCE USE DISORDER

AKA: Addiction, substance abuse, alcoholism

How it feels: While you are getting high or drunk, your brain says, "Hey, this is awesome, let's do it again." So you do it again. And again. Your brain keeps saying, "More, please!!" and you give in to the urge. You want to say, "OK, brain, maybe some other time," but when you don't give your brain what it wants, you feel like shit. You know that you really should stop getting wasted because you are effing up your life, but it feels so good and not doing it feels so bad.

What it is: People drop the word addict all the time, but when you have an addiction to something, it means it has become the main focus of your life. You spend the majority of your time thinking about how to get booze, pills, whatever—or the money you need to get your next high. Everything else in your life gradually becomes less important.

Here's how it starts: When you do something that feels good, your brain's "reward system" sends your body positive feedback. You begin to crave that feeling. The more the brain gets that intoxicating, awesome feeling, the more it needs to feel that way again.

Addictions may all start the same way, but they are not created equal. You're probably not going to steal money to buy an espresso to feed your caffeine addiction. In this book, I'm sticking to the most common and dangerous addictions, the ones involved in genuine substance use disorders. These include alcohol, opiates, stimulants, sedatives, and pot. Yes, marijuana can be addictive.

Substance use disorder is the one illness that you can totally prevent. If you never drink or try drugs, you aren't going to develop an addiction to booze or drugs. Some people may drink a lot and smoke pot, maybe even try coke or pop a few painkillers, and still never become addicted. Just like all of the other mental disorders, it's all based on your biology.

What it is not: A weakness

Symptoms: If you develop at least two of these symptoms within a year, you may have an addiction:

- Feeling like you don't have control over your drug of choice. You drink, smoke, or take more of a drug than you planned. You try to cut down but can't. You crave the substance and spend a lot of time trying to get some so you can get drunk or high again.

- Slacking off at school or work because you are high or hung over

- Coming into conflict with the people in your life because you are messed up or focused on getting high or drunk again

- Knowing that you are drinking or using too much and that it's making your health and life worse, *but doing it anyway*

- Needing to drink, smoke, or take more and more of a substance to feel the way you felt when you first started

Who gets it: Addiction is super common. About thirty million people have a drug or alcohol habit worthy of a diagnosis—that's almost one in ten of all Americans. Men used to make up the majority of addicts, but women are catching up. Fast.

How to deal: 💭 🎯 👪 🏫 ➕ 🛋 👭

Good to know: Some substances that can be legally obtained—alcohol, prescription painkillers, synthetic marijuana—are the most addictive and can be the most damaging if abused.

VIPs who have talked about being in recovery from addiction: Bradley Cooper, Dax Shepard, Kat Von D, Macklemore, Nicole Richie

MAYA'S ADVENTURE

I began using prescription painkillers (aka opioids) when I was thirteen, although I didn't have a prescription and wasn't in any pain, at least not physically. By the time I was a freshman in high school I had developed a physical dependency to the pills, which meant that I had to keep using more, more, more—not only to keep getting high but to avoid becoming sick from withdrawal.

It led to an overdose on Vicodin. Itching, vomiting, shaking, aching, and unable to urinate, I was taken to the emergency room. I was very lucky that I was able to leave the emergency room alive that night. The nurses gave me lots of water to detox my body and made me stay there for hours until they were sure I was medically stable. The overdose was actually due to liver damage I had from all the acetaminophen (the real name for Tylenol) that was in the opioid pills I was taking. I was fourteen and had liver damage!

I spent the next two years in rehab. I went to wilderness rehab in the Utah desert and then to a residential program in Salt Lake City. (You'll find more about Maya's stint in rehab in part seven.) I learned a lot about why I used, who I was, and what I wanted from recovery.

During treatment I was introduced to the idea that addiction was a chronic disease, I worried that it meant I would be struggling with it for the rest of my life. But once I started my recovery process, I reached a point where I wasn't struggling to stay off opioids. I accepted that I had an illness but that I didn't have to be sick anymore because I had the tools to manage it. My mistake was in believing that I had somehow "arrived" and could stop using those tools—that no thoughts, urges, or cravings would ever come again. Because they did.

I ended up picking up heroin after being clean for two years. Heroin took me down pretty hard. I came close to ODing several times. While I was using, I was a slave to the drug. I risked my life by going out to dangerous places by myself to cop dope off the streets and risked going to jail after being caught with a bag of heroin in the South End of Boston. I had made up my mind that I would die a miserable junkie and surrendered to a lifestyle of dishonesty, crime, and self-neglect.

Relapses are pretty common, but they're not a necessary part of recovery. It has the potential to lead to death, jail, or other major consequences—but there is no shame in a relapse.

"There is no shame in relapse. The most important thing is if and how you get back up."

The most important thing is if and how you get back up. After my first relapse, I started taking a monthly Vivitrol shot. Vivitrol is an opioid blocker that's supposed to stop you from getting high for twenty-eight days after the dose. I was still using other drugs, and near the end of the month, I attempted to override the shot by using a lot more heroin that I usually would. That turned out to be very dangerous because, although Vivitrol blocks opioids to a certain extent, a strong enough dose can break through and cause an overdose. I don't know if I would be alive if it weren't for that shot.

People say a lot of things when you're in recovery, like, "Keep fighting!" and, "You can win this battle!" To me, these phrases have undertones of force and willpower, ironically two things that are not enough to sustain recovery. For a long time, I believed that I had to struggle and fight against my disease. I'd be motivated for a little while, but then I'd become worn out and give up. Now I know that fighting wasn't the answer; I needed to surrender.

I'm in a really good place today. I see a therapist and attend a twelve-step program. Plus, I take medication to manage my depression and anxiety. I practice mindfulness and meditation and try to do something every day that brings me joy and a sense of accomplishment, like swimming, singing, writing songs, or making art. Most importantly, I ask for help when I need it, even when I'm scared that it will make me look weak.

HOW DID THIS HAPPEN?!

You might be looking for the reason that you are suffering from one of the disorders. Fair enough—but first of all, don't blame the way your parents raised you. It may be their fault that you have a hard-to-pronounce name, but after decades of research into how parenting affects the brain, there's no proof that your mom and dad created your mental illness— at least not all on their own. Research has shown that the environment matters, so parents that do a shitty job taking care of their kids (think abuse and abandonment) are making them more vulnerable. However, there are plenty of people with mental illness who grew up in super-supportive and loving homes.

So, what causes mental illness? No one knows for sure (sorry), but scientists have figured out that it is a combination of genetic, biological, and environmental factors.

GENETIC FACTORS

Since one-in-five people deal with a mental illness, you'll probably find it somewhere on your family tree. In some families, there are more people with a mental disorder than without. That's why researchers believe that mental illness can be passed down through our genes, which are also responsible for how we look and for some of our behavioral tendencies. In fact, they have identified a variation in one gene that has been linked to five disorders, including major depression, schizophrenia, bipolar disorder, autism, and attention-deficit/hyperactivity disorder (ADHD). This doesn't mean that everyone with that specific gene variation will develop a disorder, but it's a big discovery that will hopefully lead scientists to finding a clear cause someday.

Biological Factors

Your brain is filled with chemicals called neurotransmitters. They are like little walkie-talkies that help nerve cells communicate with one another. If the neurotransmitters are out of whack or unbalanced, the messages can't get through the brain. That's where the term "chemical imbalance" comes from.

Environmental Factors

By *environmental,* I'm not talking about global warming. Having a stressful childhood or being a victim of violence can create a psychological environment where mental illness can grow. There is a saying that "genetics loads the gun, but environment pulls the trigger." That means you may have inherited the brain chemistry that could lead to a particular disorder, but need something to happen in your life to actually bring it into being. This is similar to a case where someone has a genetic predisposition to heart disease and then becomes a smoker, setting herself up for a heart attack.

PART TWO

MASTER YOUR MENTAL HEALTH CARE

Imagine if people with broken ankles were limping around on one foot because they didn't know where to find a doctor. What if half of all pregnant women didn't see an OBGYN before they gave birth because they thought they could handle their pregnancy on their own? What if people with cancer decided not to get chemotherapy because they didn't have time?

It sounds ridiculous, but those are all real reasons why fewer than half of all people with a mental illness get treatment. In a recent survey by the Substance Abuse and Mental Health Services Administration, these are the excuses people gave for not seeing a therapist or trying medication, even though they knew they had a mental illness:

"I couldn't afford treatment."

"I thought I could handle it on my own."

"I didn't know where to go."

"I didn't have time."

"My insurance didn't pay enough."

"I didn't think treatment would help."

"I was concerned about being sent to a mental hospital."

"I didn't want people to have a negative opinion of me."

"I didn't want anyone to find out."

"I thought it might have a negative effect on my job."

You would probably never list these as reasons to avoid *medical* care because you have a general idea of how the health care system works—but when it comes to *mental* health care, lots of people are in the dark. So, before I bust up the reasons people often give for not getting treatment, it's essential to understand how the whole thing works.

Although psychiatry is a late bloomer in the world of medicine, by now doctors and drugmakers have developed a wide range of evidence-based therapies and medications to keep mental illness under control. That doesn't mean you can take a magical pill and call it a day. For some people, myself included, antidepressants and antipsychotic meds can seem pretty magical after years of feeling terrible, but they almost always work better when combined with therapy. *Evidence-based treatments* mean that the therapy or medication has been well-researched and proven to get positive results.

While some people only take medication and others just talk it out, the pros agree that for most people, the best treatment is medication *plus* some form of talk therapy. Think of it like dieting and working out. Each can help you slim down, but they work better together.

WHO'S WHO IN MENTAL HEALTH CARE

Thanks to urgent-care facilities and pop-up health clinics, most of us have never had to try very hard to find a doctor. As long as they are professional, ask the right questions, and listen to concerns, it doesn't matter as much who checks your blood pressure or writes you an Rx for an antibiotic.

Mental health care isn't as simple. Psychiatrists, psychologists, and other pros are trained to recognize symptoms, but since there are no basic vital signs to check, talking is the only tool they have to make a diagnosis, and it's one of the essential parts of treatment.

So, when you need to find a mental health professional, you want someone you can trust with your deepest and darkest thoughts, who you believe can understand what you're feeling, and whose opinions and advice you'll actually follow. You may need to find one who can prescribe medication, and you'll want to consider those who practice the type of therapy that will best help you. If you have a psychiatrist prescribing medication and a therapist doing therapy, you'll want to make sure they are connected so they can work together.

For better or worse, finding the right mental health pro can feel a lot like dating. Some people luck out by really liking the first one they meet. Others go from session to session looking for that special someone who gets them, practices the type of therapy they need, and has just the right opening in his schedule for convenient appointments. There is no Tinder for therapists— yet—but this guide decodes the fancy letters behind the names of mental health professionals, and should help you figure out where to start your search.

PSYCHIATRISTS

Their MO: Psychiatrists went to medical school and then did a four-year residency in psychiatry, so they are good at diagnosing patients. Since they have the power to prescribe meds, that's a big part of what they do.

Letters: MD

What they do: Diagnose mental disorders, prescribe medication, therapy sessions

What they don't: Some psychiatrists focus on finding the right diagnosis and medication and leave the weekly therapy sessions to another professional.

Where to find them: In private offices, probably with a couch and a copy of the *DSM-5*

PSYCHOLOGISTS

Their MO: Clinical psychologists spend their time doing one-on-one or group therapy with patients. They have slightly different credentials, based on the specifics of their graduate program or specialty.

Letters: PhD, PsyD, EdD

What they do: Therapy sessions

What they don't: Prescribe medication

Where to find them: In private offices with waiting rooms filled with magazines

Social Workers

Their MO: Social workers are the invisible glue that holds our society together. They work in schools, hospitals, and organizations to help people get through challenges and hard times. Many become therapists. The fee you pay to a social worker who does one-on-one therapy will probably be lower than that of a psychologist or psychiatrist.

Letters: MSW, LMSW, LCSW

What they do: Therapy sessions, case management

What they don't: Prescribe medication

Where to find them: Taking care of everyone's business at hospitals, community mental health centers, addiction treatment centers, schools, and government agencies

Counselors

Their MO: Counselors are trained to diagnose and treat mental, behavioral, and emotional problems with various types of therapy. They often specialize in dealing with topics such as addiction and marriage.

Letters: LPC, LMHC

What they do: Therapy sessions

What they don't: Prescribe medication

Where to find them: In private offices, probably with a box of tissues just in case

PRIMARY CARE PHYSICIANS

Their MO: The doctor who checks your blood pressure and gives you a physical every year can also talk to you about your mental health, but probably just for a few minutes. Physicians understand that mental and physical health are connected, and are allowed to prescribe psychiatric medication, but they don't have the time or training do therapy sessions with you.

Letters: MD

What they do: Prescribe medication, make referrals to therapists

What they don't: Therapy sessions, diagnosis mental disorders

Where to find them: Private offices or health clinics, with stethoscopes around their necks

PHYSICIAN ASSISTANT OR NURSE PRACTITIONER

Their MO: Physician assistants and nurse practitioners have enough medical training to do physical check-ups and write prescriptions, making them less authoritative than doctors—but they tend to be better listeners and might have a little more time to spend with you than an MD. They won't be able to go deep into your issues, but talking to one of them can be a great place to start your search for help.

Letters: PA and NP

What they do: Prescribe medication, make referrals to therapists

What they don't: Therapy sessions

Where to find them: Dressed in scrubs at private offices or health clinics

Psychiatric Nurse/Mental Health Nurse Practitioner

Their MO: These nurses are like a Swiss Army knife without the sharp edges. They tend to combine the calm and caring style of a nurse with advanced training in mental health. They can diagnose a mental illness, come up with a treatment plan, provide therapy, and prescribe medication.

Letters: APRN, PNP

What they do: Prescribe medication, crisis intervention, therapy sessions

What they don't: Ongoing therapy

Where to find them: Pulling a twelve-hour shift at a hospital or treatment center

FAITH LEADER

Their MO: Some faith leaders have training in clinical pastoral education, which means they are trained to provide individual and group counseling. Expect a big emphasis on God.

Letters: AAPC

What they do: Therapy sessions

What they don't: Prescribe medication

Where to find them: In a church, synagogue, or other house of worship

SCHOOL COUNSELOR

Their MO: School counselors have training similar to that of social workers and counselors, and are dedicated to helping students from kindergarten through twelfth grade. They may be more focused on helping you get into college than dealing with your depression, but they are a smart place to start when you need support.

Letters: Nada, but they need a state license

What they do: Make referrals to therapists

What they don't: Therapy sessions, prescribe medication

Where to find them: Schools

FIND A THERAPIST WHO GETS YOU

Now that you have some idea of what the mental health professionals do, it's time to start your search for the one that fits your needs.

1) Cast a wide net.

Ask around to see if anyone in your circle has someone to recommend, call your insurer for a list of in-network pros, or go online. There are dozens of websites that list counselors by location and specialty, but, as in the digital-dating world, all sites aren't created equal. These legit sites are all worth your time: www.Helppro.com, www.Psychologytoday.com, and www.Zocdoc.com. As you ask and scroll around, compile a running list of maybes.

2) Make the first move.

Once you have your list of five to ten potential therapists, you need to find out who is available, aka, accepting new patients. At this point, you're more interested in finding out if they can work with your schedule and budget, not about establishing a deep connection.

If you are using your medical insurance to pay for therapy, be sure to ask if they accept your plan. (If that's the case, you'll probably want to start with a longer list of possibilities, since many therapists don't take insurance.) The simplest way to do this is by sending a quick e-mail letting them know a little bit about yourself and what you are looking for in a therapist. Something like this should do the trick:

"Hi. I'm Ashley, and I'm interested in seeing a therapist to help me manage my symptoms of depression and anxiety. Right now, I am only available to come in for evening and weekend appointments. I would like to use my insurance, which is UnitedHealthcare PPO. If that would work for you, please let me know. I look forward to hearing from you."

3) Set up a phone date.

Once you've identified a few professionals who seem promising, it's time to find out how comfortable you feel talking to them. The best way to do this is to schedule a call with the potential matches. Ideally, you want to chat with at least three.

On the call, ask each one about his or her experience and specialties, and be prepared to share what you want to accomplish in therapy. Although it's faster and may be less intimidating, resist the temptation to ask your questions over e-mail. This call is necessary to determine if you have chemistry with the therapist and will be able to share your thoughts and feelings when you meet.

4) Meet IRL.

By now, you should have a pretty good idea of which therapists you want to meet. Most offer a free initial interview or fifteen-minute session before you commit to your first session.

BTW, trying to make your therapist happy or get him to like you is not the point of therapy. (Unless of course, needing everyone to like you is something you want to work on in therapy.)

You want to feel like you can trust this person with your deepest darkest secrets, though, and you also need to feel comfortable in the office (or with the video chat set-up, if that is your thing).

5) Go steady, but don't commit.

Therapy is not about seeing one person once a week for the rest of your life. Tell your therapist you'd like to work on [insert issue here] for three to six months. A therapy goal might include how you want to feel, relationships you want to work on, or something you want to achieve in your life. Having a few goals and a timeline will help keep both of you on track. A good therapist will help you work toward your goals and maybe suggest new ones.

6) Don't ghost the rejects.

It's hard out there for a therapist. Send a super short e-mail to everyone you speak with on the phone or in person—including the rejects. It can be as simple as, *"Thanks for your time. I'm going to begin therapy with someone else."*

7) Set check-in points to make sure therapy is still working for you.

When you are upfront about what you want to accomplish in therapy, it makes it a heck of a lot easier to talk about your goals along the way. But even if you didn't, every few months, ask yourself what you still want to work on. Keep going until you can't answer that question anymore, or no longer feel your therapist can help you get there.

THERAPIES THAT WORK

Retail therapy and massage therapy, which sadly are not evidence-based treatments, are universally the most enjoyable types of therapy. *Real* therapy—where you share your darkest thoughts, work through painful memories, and learn to cope with difficult symptoms—is not always going to be fun. Sometimes it might it even suck. That is often when the breakthroughs happen, so try to stick with it.

There are many different types of therapy, and you should try as many as you feel comfortable with until you find the one that works best for you. Below, I've described ten evidence-based therapies proven to help those of us with a mental disorder.

PSYCHOTHERAPY 🛋

What it is: Known as "talk therapy" or straight-up "counseling," psychotherapy is what most of us think of when we think of therapy. It's you and a therapist talking about your issues. The therapist may use a specific combination of therapies, including interpersonal therapy, which helps you deal with other people; and problem-solving therapy, where you figure out how to deal with everything else in life.

Who it helps: Practically every human on earth

Pro to see: Psychiatrist, psychologist, social worker, counselor, or faith leader

How often: The standard schedule is once a week, but you should feel free to book more sessions if you need them. It's a good idea to start with a three or six-month goal, so your therapist knows you are focused on working through your issues.

COGNITIVE BEHAVIORAL THERAPY (CBT) ○

What it is: This type of therapy can help you understand how your thoughts are connected to your actions. During CBT, a therapist helps you figure out why some of your ideas and beliefs make you feel bad or act a certain way. She will start out by asking you questions to figure out which ways of thinking are creating a problem in your life. Then she can help you learn what triggers those thoughts and feelings—and how to change them. By the end, you will have retrained your brain to guard against those negative thoughts and self-destructive patterns.

Who it helps: If there could be only one therapy style to help to help everyone with a mental illness, this would be it. To make it work for you, you'll have to be motivated to make changes and do some homework assignments, such as keeping a journal. CBT isn't one-size-fits-all. It's designed to be specific to your thoughts and behaviors.

Pro to see: Psychiatrist, psychologist, social worker, or counselor trained in CBT

How often: CBT is highly structured. You aren't going to go in a shoot the shit for a half hour and be done with it. The whole process usually takes ten-to-twenty-four weekly sessions. Plus homework.

Good to know: You can do CBT online.

Dialectical Behavior Therapy (DBT) 🎯

What it is: DBT is a type of CBT that can help you replace negative thoughts and self-destructive behaviors with new coping skills, including mindfulness, regulating emotions, accepting reality, and tolerating distress. You'll meet with a therapist to discuss how your thoughts and beliefs are creating a problem in your life. Plus, you'll attend daily or weekly group sessions where you learn essential DBT skills and talk about how to apply them to your life. Be prepared to have homework and check-ins with your DBT leader in between sessions. By the end, you will have a new set of skills to help you deal with your negative thoughts and break your self-destructive patterns.

Who it helps: DBT was created for people with borderline personality disorder, but can also help those dealing with bipolar disorder and substance use disorder.

Pro to see: A psychologist, social worker, or counselor trained in DBT

How often: DBT is intense. You'll need to invest a few hours a week in a therapy session and group meeting, plus make time for homework. Treatment can last anywhere from twenty weeks to a year.

GROUP THERAPY 👭

What it is: When you think of group therapy, you may be picturing an AA meeting or a cancer survivors' support group. Although the basic idea of peers supporting one another in dealing with a specific issue such as grief, anger, or addiction is the same, group therapy is led by a mental health pro who guides the group through a particular type of therapy. The group usually consists of six to twelve people who want to help one another understand and deal with their problems, which could mean calling someone out for her BS. The therapist leading the group uses the techniques of psychotherapy, interpersonal therapy, or CBT, and helps members talk through their issues and see their strengths and weaknesses.

Who it helps: There are lots of disorder-specific groups, especially for anxiety, eating disorders, and substance use disorder.

Pro to see: Social workers shine here because they tend to know how to manage group dynamics and make sure that everyone is following the rules and working together.

How often: Groups usually meet weekly and sometimes have a start and end date. They might go on for anywhere from six weeks to a year.

FAMILY THERAPY 👪

What it is: Based on the idea that a supportive family is your best asset, family therapy is kind of like talk therapy for the whole family. In family therapy, the therapist tries to get every person to speak openly and honestly so they can best support the person who is struggling. He'll use interpersonal therapy and problem-solving therapy to help create a better home environment for everyone. If your family is super dysfunctional, don't bother. It isn't that your family is beyond repair—it's just that getting them all together in a therapist's office may not help *you*.

Who it helps: People with substance use disorder or eating disorder most often benefit from family therapy, but anyone with a supportive family may find it useful.

Pro to see: It's critical that the therapist has never done individual therapy with anyone in your family. That's because a therapist puts their patient's needs first and wouldn't be able to be unbiased towards everyone else in the family. Some therapists have specialized training in family therapy, but any psychologist, social worker, counselor, or faith leader with experience working with families could do it.

How often: Anywhere from two to ten weekly sessions

EYE-MOVEMENT DESENSITIZATION AND REPROCESSING (EMDR) ◦ ◦

What it is: The theory behind EMDR is that some memories of traumatic experiences have never been entirely processed, and remain stored in your mind. Since these stored memories are linked to trauma, they can impact the way you react to other negative—though not necessarily traumatic—experiences. During an EMDR session, the therapist helps you tap into your stored memories and describe traumatic images while receiving sensory input such as side-to-side eye movements.

Who it helps: People with PTSD and others who have experienced trauma

Pro to see: Psychologist, social worker, or counselor trained in EMDR

How often: There are several phases of EMDR, so it will probably take a few sixty-to-ninety-minute visits to complete one session. Studies have shown effectiveness after a few weeks of EMDR sessions.

Exposure Therapy 🔍

What it is: Many people avoid certain things, situations and activities in order to reduce their symptoms. This approach works in the short term, but over time it can make the fear even worse. Exposure therapy allows people to confront their fears in a safe environment. In exposure therapy, your psychologist will expose you to things you are afraid of, whether IRL, through your imagination, or by using virtual reality.

Who it helps: People with generalized anxiety disorder, social anxiety disorder, panic disorder, PTSD, and OCD

Pro to see: Psychologist you feel really comfortable with

How often: It really depends on the individual, but sessions typically take place during or in place of a therapy sessions.

TRANSCRANIAL MAGNETIC STIMULATION (TMS) 💀

What it is: TMS is a procedure that uses magnetic fields to stimulate the brain in effort to reduce symptoms of depression and improve mood. It's usually tried after someone hasn't responded to, or can't take, antidepressants. During TMS an electromagnetic coil, which looks like an electronic sweatband or a space helmet, is placed on your forehead. The electromagnet delivers a pulse that stimulates the nerve cells in your brain that control mood.

Who it helps: TMS has been proven to reduce symptoms of depression, bipolar disorder, schizophrenia, and schizoaffective disorder

Pro to see: A psychiatrist and a physician

How often: People typically have repetitive sessions of TMS, aka rTMS. Sessions last about forty minutes and are carried out five days each week for a period or four to six weeks.

Good to know: TMS isn't always covered by insurance.

ELECTROCONVULSIVE THERAPY (ECT) ⚡

What it is: ECT, aka "shock therapy," is a medical procedure where tiny electrical currents give the brain a brief seizure. ECT changes the brain's chemistry and has been shown to reverse depression and mania. Your psychiatrist and medical doc will run a few tests to determine whether ECT is right for you. If it is, you will then have your ECT session or sessions at a hospital, under general anesthesia. While you are knocked out, the medical team will make an electric current pass through your brain, causing you to have a sixty-second seizure. Once in recovery, the anesthesia will gradually wear off, and your medical team will monitor your symptoms.

Who it helps: People with severe depression, bipolar disorder, schizophrenia, and schizoaffective disorder who haven't responded to medication or other treatments (or can't take meds due to other concerns such as pregnancy).

Pro to see: Psychiatrist

How often: Patients typically undergo two to three ECT sessions each week for two or three weeks. After six sessions, they usually have fewer symptoms.

Good to know: ECT has a bad rap because back in the day docs used too much electricity and left out the anesthesia. It caused memory loss and understandably freaked-out patients. It is much, much safer today.

LIGHT THERAPY ☼

What it is: By *light*, I don't mean *a little bit* of therapy. Light therapy involves sitting near a special light that is brighter than conventional indoor lighting but not as bright as sunlight. This sends a signal to your brain to "lighten up" (pun intended) and can ease symptoms of depression.

Who it helps: People with seasonal affective disorder and other types of depression.

Pro to see: None—you can order a light therapy lamp online and follow the directions.

How often: Check the Center for Environmental Therapies website, www.Cet.org, to find out exactly how much light therapy you need.

QUIZ: IS ONLINE THERAPY RIGHT FOR YOU?

1. How much time are you putting into self-care these days?

A. My mental health is my number-one priority right now, so I'm a 24/7 self-care machine.

B. I could probably squeeze in some more time in between my weekly yoga session and fifteen-minute meditations.

C. Is that a joke? I'm lucky to be reading this book.

2. When all your friends tell you about a new app, you:

A. Zone out. I'm perfectly content to use my phone to talk and text, thank you.

B. Lean in. I've been meaning to take a trip to the App Store.

C. Yawn. That app had its moment at SXSW two years ago.

3. Fill-in-the-blank: FaceTime is _____.

A. When you finally get to speak to someone face-to-face, like over coffee.

B. The iPhone version of Skype.

C. The way I talk to basically everyone I know. How else would they get to see my #iwokeuplikethis face?

4. When you need to find a quiet, private space at home, where do you head?

A. Ha! Does my closet count?

B. It's tough when parents or roommates are home, but I can probably find a time when I have the place to myself.

C. Anywhere I want. You can hear a pin drop in this place.

5. What are you most looking for in a therapist?

A. Someone with a prescription pad.

B. Someone I trust and respect.

C. Someone who can be there for me whenever, wherever.

Mostly As: One of the most important parts of therapy is feeling comfortable enough to open up and dive into your issue. If you feel awkward talking to a tiny version of a person on a screen or don't have privacy at home, you will be happier and more successful seeing a therapist in her cozy space.

Mostly Bs: Sounds like you have the whole tech thing down. If you don't have time for waiting-room magazine reading, much less a commute, and aren't looking for someone to keep you in meds, give online therapy a try.

Mostly Cs: Is your dream to have a tiny therapist in your pocket, guiding your every move? Or is FaceTime just the only way you'll be able to see a therapist. Lucky for you, there's an app for that. As long as you don't need your therapist to prescribe meds—and most of us don't—online therapy may be for you.

SHIT PEOPLE SAY ABOUT MEDICATION

Psychiatric meds are probably the most misunderstood pharmaceuticals in the history of medicine. Let's get the most common myths out of the way.

"Meds make you suicidal."

There is no evidence that taking an antidepressant will bring on thoughts of suicide. However, studies have found that people, especially teens, who were *already* thinking about death might think about it more on meds, and may even try to take their own life.

"Meds change your personality."

Medications won't change who you love or what TV shows you like to binge-watch. Taken correctly, they will take away the symptoms of your illness just like any other medication would. Think about them as if they were Tylenol. Is having a headache part of your personality? No. Even if your symptoms have been a constant in your life, your anxiety, mania, or depression are not who you are.

"Meds are addictive."

Most psychiatric medications do cause withdrawal symptoms such as headaches, nausea, or insomnia if you stop taking them suddenly. That isn't the same as addiction. If you want to quit, your psychiatrist can help you come up with a plan to slowly taper off, so you don't go into withdrawal.

"Meds make you uncreative."

This is one of the hardest myths to disprove because creativity is so subjective. We do have stories from hundreds of creative types who credit their body of work to medications that quelled their anxiety and lifted the dark cloud of depression—and plenty of artists who didn't take them and died too soon.

"Once you start to feel better, you can stop taking meds."

Keep in mind that you started to feel better *because* of the medication. That was the whole point. It's usually not a good idea to stop taking something that is working for you, but if you find yourself wanting to quit, talk to your doctor about it.

"You can't take antidepressants when you are pregnant."

If you are likely to have an episode of depression during pregnancy or right after your baby is born, my personal opinion (remember, I'm not an MD) is that you can and should stay on your antidepressants. There is a small risk of lower birth weight and developmental delays in your child, but untreated depression during pregnancy can be much worse for both mom and baby causing miscarriages, serious complications, and even suicide. But don't take my word for it; your obstetrician and psychiatrist (or a reproductive psychiatrist if you can find one) can help you make the right decision for you and your baby.

"Name-brand drugs are better than generic ones."

Nope. Generics have the same mix of chemicals, just no bad TV commercials.

"You can't ever drink while taking antidepressants."

You can thank lawyers for perpetuating this myth via a warning on every pill bottle stating, "DO NOT DRINK ALCOHOL." They get paid to think about the worst-case scenarios. Here's the deal: Take it slow until you know how the meds will impact you. Then, drink in moderation. (And of course, never drink and drive.)

THE PSYCHIATRIC MEDICINE CABINET

There's a lot of noise out there about what meds you should or shouldn't take from advertising, friends, and know-it-all moms. There's one person you should listen to above all the rest: a doctor you trust. This quickie guide to the different types of psychiatric medications is not medical advice. It's here to give you a better understanding of how meds work, and what to think about and ask when your doc whips out the prescription pad.

ANTIDEPRESSANTS

Despite their name, these aren't just for depression. There are four different types of antidepressants that work to relieve symptoms of anxiety, OCD, and eating disorders. SSRIs are the most popular by far, but there are other options for people who don't respond to them.

Selective serotonin reuptake inhibitors (SSRIs)

Brand names: Celexa, Lexapro, Luvox, Paxil, Prozac, Zoloft

How they work: SSRIs are the most commonly prescribed class of antidepressants. They increase the brain's level of serotonin.

Tricyclic antidepressants (TCAs)

Brand names: Amitriptyline, Clomipramine, Desipramine, Doxepin, Imipramine, Nortriptyline, Protriptyline, Trimipramine

How they work: These older antidepressants block the reuptake of serotonin and norepinephrine which control mood and stress.

Because they involve a broader approach to balancing the chemicals, they typically have more side effects.

Monoamine oxidase inhibitors (MAOIs)

Brand names: Emsam, Marplan, Nardil, Parnate

How they work: These are the oldest antidepressants of the bunch. But because they can cause serious side effects when they interact with things containing tyramine—including cheese, chocolate, wine, and beer—they are nobody's favorite.

Good to know: You need to wait at least five weeks after taking an SSRI before trying an MAOI because combining them can be dangerous.

Atypical antidepressants

Known as: Aplenzin, Forfivo XL, Trintellix, Remeron, Wellbutrin

How they work: These are called *atypical antidepressants* because they target other chemicals in the brain, either alone or along with serotonin.

ANTIPSYCHOTICS

The name is a little harsh, but these meds are designed to prevent the "psychotic" symptoms of schizophrenia, schizoaffective disorder, bipolar disorder, and severe depression. The first generation of these meds has been known to cause neurological disorders and diabetes. The second generation, atypical antipsychotics, are improved and can be taken in liquid or shot form as well as pill form.

First-generation typical antipsychotics

Brand names: Haldol, Navane, Prolixin, Thorazine, Trilafon

How they work: These drugs block dopamine receptors and can affect levels of other chemicals, including serotonin, acetylcholine, and noradrenaline, which effects behavior, mood, and emotion.

Second-generation atypical antipsychotics

Brand names: Abilify, Geodon, Risperdal, Saphris, Seroquel, Ziprasidone, Zyprexa

How they work: Like their first-generation predecessors, these antipsychotics block receptor's to the brain's dopamine pathways—without all of the negative side effects.

MOOD STABILIZERS

These meds work to suppress mood shifts between depression and mania. They are commonly prescribed for bipolar disorder.

Brand names: Carbotrol, Depakene, Depakote Sprinkle, Lamictal, Lithium, Tegretol

How they work: Although each one works a little differently, these mood stabilizers were all designed to change with the levels of chemicals in the brain.

REASONS TO AVOID TREATMENT—REVISITED

Remember that list of reasons people give for staying away from treatment? It should be clear at this point that they don't hold up once you have the facts. So, if someone tries one of these excuses on you, hit them with one of these comebacks. Even better— hand them a copy of this book.

"I can't afford treatment."

There are tons of places that allow you to pay on a sliding scale, and if you are totally broke the government can chip in.

"I think I can handle it on my own."

Are you willing to bet your happiness and your life on it?

"I don't know where to go."

Start with your regular doctor or search, www.Helppro.com, www.Psychologytoday.com, and www.Zocdoc.com.

"I don't have time."

You can see an online therapist from your couch, on your schedule.

"My insurance doesn't pay enough."

You may be able to change your insurance to a plan with more generous benefits.

"I don't think treatment will help."

There are so many kinds of treatment out there that have been proven to work. You can't know unless you try.

"I'm concerned about being sent to a mental hospital."

The only reason you'd be involuntarily hospitalized is if you are considered to be an immediate danger to yourself or someone else—in which case, hospitalization is probably a good idea.

"I don't want people to have a negative opinion of me."

Getting support is a good thing, and your real friends won't judge you for it—but keep in mind that your conversations with medical professionals will all be confidential. There's no reason anyone has to know you are getting help unless you want them to.

"I don't want anyone to find out."

HIPAA has you covered. It is the privacy law that makes it illegal for anyone to share your medical records without your written consent.

"I think it might have a negative effect on my job."

Being mentally healthy will make you a better employee.

PART THREE

ALL ABOUT THE BILLS

Health care is a hot mess right now. Americans spend more than any other country in the world on their medical bills, but we rank toward the bottom of all industrialized nations in health outcomes. We're basically paying for a shiny new Mercedes-Benz and getting a Honda that doesn't run very well. And it isn't just that we aren't getting our money's worth. Unlike our friends in Canada, Europe, and Australia, millions of our citizens don't have access to health care at all.

This part of the book focuses on how you can pay for psychiatrists, therapists, and medication on your budget. I'll also explain different types of insurance, and how to get the care you need, even when you are totally broke.

GET THE BEST INSURANCE FOR YOUR BUDGET

It all starts with your insurance plan. *Health insurance* is a pretty dumb thing to call it. Unlike car insurance or renter's insurance, which you hope you'll never need, everyone expects to use their health insurance when they go to a doctor. It's actually health *coverage*—but, to keep it simple, I'll keep calling it *insurance*.

There are about a zillion different types of insurance, but most fall into a few categories. Private insurance is either sponsored by an employer or employer group (such as a union or WeWork) or purchased off of the Health Insurance Marketplace, also often called Obamacare. Public insurance and assistance, known as Medicaid and Medicare, are sponsored by the government, and the military funds Tricare.

As currently mandated by the Affordable Care Act, all plans cover doctor visits, hospital stays, and offer essential health benefits that include screening for depression and alcohol misuse. Insurers aren't allowed to charge more to cover mental health or addiction services, discriminate against people with pre-existing conditions, or set limits on how much health care you can use in your lifetime.

For each plan, you pay a monthly fee called a *premium*. There is also a *deductible* you have to pay down before your insurance kicks in. Some plans count your *co-pay*—the amount of money you have to kick in at the time of a doctor visit—toward your deductible. Co-pays tend to range from $25 to $75.

All of this can be overwhelming—especially if number-crunching isn't your thing. Investing a few hours in figuring out your insurance options is one of the best things you can do for your mental health and your bank account.

Here's how the plans work:

EMPLOYER-BASED INSURANCE

What it is: Companies with fifty or more employees are required to offer health insurance, although they don't have to pay for it. Most employers cover some of the premiums, and a precious few pay the whole tab for their employees. (That's a pretty luxe benefit, and something to consider when you're job hunting.)

Companies make a deal with a large insurance provider such as Aetna or United Healthcare and usually give its employees a few options of plans, so they can pick what works best for them and their families. Under the Affordable Care Act, parents are allowed to cover their children until they turn twenty-six. The cost of the plan depends on how much coverage you get.

Each insurance company has a list of go-to doctors in their *network*. These are the people who say yes when you ask, "Do you accept my insurance?" Many plans allow you to see any provider but charge you more for these "out of network" benefits.

Options may include:

- **High-deductible health plan (HDHP):** These plans have low monthly premiums and higher deductibles, so you end up paying out-of-pocket for doctor visits, but if something major goes wrong, they've got you covered. They are a cheapie option if you don't think you'll need to see a doc much.

- **Point of service (POS):** Behind the scenes, insurance companies make deals with hospitals, clinics, doctors, and mental health pros (who they call *providers*) to get a lower rate for people on their plan. It's kind of like a friends-and-family discount. Going *in-network*—using doctors listed as part of the plan—limits the selection of pros you can choose from, but you'll only have to hand over a co-pay. You'll need to see your primary care doc for a referral before going to a specialist, such as a psychiatrist.

- **Health maintenance organization (HMO):** HMOs were created to keep costs low for everyone. They are similar to POS plans, but the network is made up of doctors who work for your insurance company. These plans are a great value if you aren't attached to your docs and therapist because they may not be in your HMO group.

- **Exclusive provider organization (EPO):** You pay a decent chunk of change to the doctors in your insurance's "exclusive provider" network, which is typically a lot wider than what you'd get with a POS or HMO plan.

- **Preferred provider organization (PPO):** These plans have a higher premium, but you get to go to any doctor you want without a referral. #Merica

Who can get it: Anyone who works for a company with fifty-plus employees, along with their husbands/wives/domestic partners and children under the age of twenty-six.

How to sign up: See your HR department as soon as you start a new job and don't be afraid to ask alllll the questions.

How much it costs: The average price of a premium for an individual was $110 per month in 2016, but costs vary widely and depend on how much, if anything, the company is kicking in.

Pros: In general, these are the best plans because employers pay an average of eighty percent of the total tab for singles and seventy percent for families.

Cons: You have no control over which plan(s) your company offers.

Individual Insurance (aka, Obamacare)

What it is: It's hard to believe, but before the Affordable Care Act, it was really hard for freelancers, entrepreneurs, and people who didn't have access to an employer or government-sponsored plan to buy insurance. Now, hundreds of companies sell insurance on the Health Insurance Marketplace. The plans can be pricey, but many states offer a tax credit on premiums, which lowers the cost in the long run.

There are four types of plans (all named after metal for some strange reason):

- **Bronze:** This is the cheapest group of plans, but be aware that the insurers cover only sixty percent of your costs. This coverage is better than nothing, but not a good deal for people managing a mental illness.

- **Silver:** You pay a low-ish monthly premium, and the insurer covers seventy percent of your costs. It's a solid plan if you see a psychiatrist and take meds on a regular basis. If your state provides subsidies to offset the cost of your premium, they require you to get this plan.

- **Gold:** These plans cost slightly more per month than silvers and cover eighty percent of your medications and doctor visits. A gold plan is a good buy if you need regular care and can work a significant insurance payment into your monthly budget.

- **Platinum:** You pay a high premium each month, which covers ninety percent of your medical expenses. If you have a chronic medical condition that requires expensive medications, or you see a doctor (besides your therapist) at least once a month, this plan is worth the price tag.

Who can get it: Any US citizen

How to sign up: Go to www.Healthcare.gov and follow the steps. During open enrollment, from November 1st to December 15th, you can enroll in a plan that will start the following January 1st. Once you are in the insurance-buying zone, it's like online shopping (although not as fun). The choices can be overwhelming, but you can take a quiz to suss out your needs or call/chat with a navigator for extra help in understanding all the options. Don't expect this to be a quick call, though.

How much it costs: The younger you are, the lower your costs will be overall. Yep, that's legal. In 2017, the average monthly premium for a thirty-year-old was $553 (Platinum), $464 (Silver), $364 (Gold), and $311 (Bronze).

Pros: You can buy your own insurance!

Cons: Many doctors won't accept patients who buy marketplace plans. Boo.

CH-CH-CHANGES

If you have an employer health insurance plan or Obamacare, you are allowed to sign up or change plans any time you experience one of these "qualifying life events":

- Make it official with your domestic partner or get married (or divorced)
- Lose your job
- Move to a different zip code, including when you go off to college
- Have a baby or adopt a child
- Lose your coverage because a parent died
- Qualify for Medicaid

Medicaid

What it is: Medicaid is an assistance program meant for people who don't make enough money to buy insurance. You may *feel* like you don't have enough money to cover your health care tab, but the government won't just take your word for it. According to them, if you make less than the federal poverty level, which is $12,000 per year for one person in 2018, you are legit broke.

Medicaid is technically a federal program, but each state gets to make up its own rules about who can get it and how much they have to pay. Most states allow people who make double the income of the federal poverty level, and some even let you triple it and still qualify for Medicaid. Google your state's Medicaid guidelines for details.

Medicaid covers doctor's visits, including sessions with a psychiatrist or therapist, and most hospital stays. There's no enrollment period, so if you qualify your coverage begins ASAP.

How to sign up: Go to www.Medicaid.gov and follow the steps.

Who can get it: People with low incomes and those who can't work because of a disability.

How much it costs: Since the point of Medicaid is to provide health care to people who couldn't otherwise afford it, it's usually free. Depending on the state you live in, you may have to make a co-pay or meet a low deductible.

Pros: It's cheap or free for people who qualify.

Cons: Medicaid reimburses doctors at a much lower rate than other insurers do, so a lot of doctors don't accept patients who are on it. It doesn't cover prescription drugs, or psychiatric hospital stays for people under twenty-one.

MEDICARE

What it is: Medicare is the health insurance plan everyone is eligible for when they turn sixty-five—but it isn't just for your grandparents. People with schizophrenia, bipolar disorder, and other disabilities can join Medicare at any age.

Medicare is a federal program, but unlike Medicaid, it is basically the same in every state. It covers doctors' visits, including sessions with a psychiatrist or therapist, and most hospital stays. Like Medicaid, there's no enrollment period, so your coverage begins as soon as you qualify.

Who can get it: Anyone who has had his or her sixty-fifth birthday and people with disabilities.

How to sign up: Go to www.Medicare.gov and follow the steps.

How much it costs: If you keep an eye on your pay stub, you may have noticed that you're forking over cash to FICA. That's a tax you pay to fund the Social Security and Medicare programs. You are required to pay into the system while you are working so you can qualify for these benefits once you retire. That's why, if you haven't racked up ten years of on-the-books work by the time you need the benefits, you pay a premium. There are four parts to

Medicare. Part A is for hospital care, B is for doctor visits, and D is for prescription drug coverage. Part C is a combo of part A and B.

Pros: Unlike Medicaid, almost all doctors and hospitals accept patients with Medicare coverage.

Cons: It's confusing to figure out which part—A, B, C, or D— you need. And those monthly premiums add up fast.

TRICARE

What it is: This is the insurance plan for veterans, people in the military, national guard, army reserve, and their families. It covers doctors' visits, including therapy sessions, medications, and hospital stays. There are several different plans you can choose from, based on your needs and whether you have access to a Military Treatment Facility. A referral or preauthorization is often required to see a specialist, including a psychiatrist.

Who can get it: Veterans and people on active duty in all branches of the military, national guard, federal reserve, and their families. If the vet or soldier dies, the family can stay on the plan.

How to sign up: Go to www.Tricare.mil and follow the steps.

How much it costs: Less than $50 a month for individual coverage and just over $200 for a family.

Pros: It's one of the most affordable plans out there.

Cons: There's a lot of paperwork, and you need to get a referral and pre-authorization for all mental health care.

HOW HEALTH CARE
BECAME A HOT MESS

The health care system didn't get this way overnight. It took a century of advancements in science, medicine, technology, and attempts by many presidents to ensure everyone could afford care.

1910s–1920s

If you were sick, you'd call a doctor to come to your house and pay him a few bucks. Since doctor bills weren't that high then, and there weren't many meds available, there was no need for health insurance.

1930–1940s

As hospitals got fancier (read: clean) and more sophisticated medications were developed, costs went up. Businesses started to pick up the tab for employees as a perk—mainly because they wanted their staff healthy so they could get back to work. Some politicians, including Presidents Roosevelt and Truman, thought everyone should have this benefit, so they sent bills to Congress with provisions for universal health care. "No can do," said Congress. Too expensive. Since ending World War II was a bigger priority for these leaders, they gave up on health care.

1950s

World War II had a massive impact on medicine, and by the time it ended, penicillin, morphine, and many life-saving techniques had been developed. Health care became a big business, which made medical bills bigger, too. Insurance companies got in the game by charging a monthly fee to cover costs.

1960s

It was becoming difficult for poor, old, and disabled people to pay their medical bills, so President Johnson passed the Medicare and Medicaid Act of 1965. It was the largest health care reform ever, but they didn't bother to crunch the numbers to see how much it would cost Americans in the long run. (Spoiler alert: A lot.)

1970s-1990s

Health care got really, really expensive and by the end of the century, sixteen percent of the population didn't have health insurance and sure as hell couldn't pay for medical care without it. There was a lot of shady stuff going down, like people being refused insurance because they had a "pre-existing condition" such as depression or asthma. In 1996, President Clinton signed the Health Insurance Portability and Accountability Act, aka HIPAA. You probably think of HIPAA as that extra form you have to sign at the doc's office saying they'll keep your stuff confidential, but it's about more than privacy. HIPAA made it illegal for insurers to deny you coverage if you have a pre-existing condition.

2000-2009

President Bush signed the Mental Health Parity and Addiction Equity Act of 2008, which was kind of like an equal-rights bill for people dealing with mental illness and addiction. It forced insurers to cover those conditions just as they would any physical illness or disability.

2010–2016

There were more people without insurance than ever before. President Obama made passing a blockbuster health care reform bill his number-one priority, and he pulled it off. In 2010, he signed the Patient Protection and Affordable Care Act (ACA), which everyone calls *Obamacare*. There is a debate on just how "affordable" it is, but it did expand Medicaid, let kids stay on their parents' plan until age twenty-six, and gave everyone else the chance to buy insurance on the Health Insurance Marketplace. Once the ACA became law, if you decided not to buy health care, you had to pay an annual fee. This pissed a lot of people off, but the Supreme Court said it was legit.

The ACA was a big win for people with mental health issues. It recognized that mental health care is an essential health benefit, and made sure that all insurance plans covered it. Depression and alcohol misuse screening was added to the list of preventive care services that everyone should have access to, just like getting your blood pressure taken.

2017–Today

President Trump and the Republican-led House and Senate put repealing the ACA at the top of their to-do list. It proved to be a harder bill to take down than expected, but they did manage to get rid of the insurance mandate so that people who decide not to have coverage don't have to pay a fine.

THERAPY YOU CAN AFFORD

Even with a great insurance plan, therapy can add up fast. Consider your all options so you can get the care you need.

Self-Pay ($$$$)

More mental health pros refuse to take insurance than any other category of health professionals. They aren't trying to be mean, just realistic. Therapy sessions usually last forty-five minutes, so a therapist can only see seven or eight clients a day, max, unlike a physician, who sometimes sees twenty patients in the same amount of time. To make up for this, they need to collect more cash for each patient they see—but insurance companies don't pay anywhere near the same rate for a therapy session as a for a specialist visit. The alternative is to skip insurance altogether and charge you directly.

Out-of-Network Providers ($$$)

There are lots of therapists who do take insurance but may not be in your plan. If you have a mental health pro you love, it might be worth paying a little more for an insurance plan with out-of-network benefits, so that at least part of the fee is covered.

In-Network Providers ($$)

Finding a therapist who takes your insurance is the dream scenario. You'll pay your typical co-pay, probably at the specialist rate. That doesn't mean the cost of sessions won't add up quickly, but it's the best deal out there.

Online Therapy ($–$$)

There are dozens of online platforms that let you chat, e-mail, and video conference with a therapist. In most cases, you can buy a package of visits, kind of like a class card at a fitness studio. Sessions can end up costing less than the co-pay with an in-network therapist. And, if you are looking for 24/7 support, the package usually includes unlimited messaging with your therapist. Since online therapy, sometimes called *e-therapy* or *telehealth,* is still a new thing, it usually isn't covered by insurance. On the plus side, you won't have to spend time or money getting to an appointment. If you want to give it a try, www.Talkspace.com, www.Mavenclinic.com, and www.Betterhelp.com are good sites.

Community Health Clinics ($)

Many local community health clinics are Federally Qualified Health Centers (FQHC), which means they get money from the government to provide health care, including therapy. They set their rates on a sliding scale, so you pay what you can afford. You can find one at www.Findahealthcenter.hrsa.gov.

University Psychology Clinic ($)

You don't have to be a student to get therapy on campus. Most colleges and universities with a psychology department have a clinic to give grad students experience practicing therapy. It's a great budget option if you don't mind seeing a newbie—and a pro almost always supervises the sessions. These clinics usually operate on a sliding scale based on your ability to pay.

EAP Counseling (Free!)

Most medium-to-large companies offer an Employee Assistance Program (EAP). The EAP is there to help employees deal with life and family issues so that they can stay focused on their work. The EAP typically includes three-to-six free counseling sessions for every employee, and sometimes their families as well. Ask HR about your EAP program. Your boss never needs to know.

Crisis Hotlines (Free!)

It's not a substitute for a therapy session, and it is definitely not a way to get a diagnosis or a prescription, but there are several hotlines and chat services that will let you connect with a counselor when you really need to talk. Add the numbers in part ten to your phone now in case you ever find yourself in need.

★ Real Talk:

Less than half of people surveyed say they can afford their health care.

HACKS TO LOWER YOUR BILLS

You don't have to be a grifter to whittle down your mental health care costs. Try one or all of these hacks, and you may end up covering your costs with loose change.

Get Free Screenings. They aren't as fun as movie screenings, but health fairs typically offer free screenings for depression, anxiety, and addiction. Think of it as a one-time, five-to-ten-minute therapy session, without the co-pay. If your screen comes up positive, you'll want to make a follow-up appointment with a pro.

See Your Therapist Every Other Week. No law says you have to see your therapist once a week, every week, for the rest of your life. If you get to a point where you feel like your issues are mostly handled, discuss cutting back on your appointments. Your therapist will probably be able to squeeze you in if you need extra sessions.

Ask Your Doc for Generic Drugs. They are almost always cheaper than their brand-name equivalents. Unlike groceries, where the store brand may not be all that, there is no secret sauce in pills. The formula is the same whether generic or branded. (Why should *you* pay for those annoying drug commercials?)

Use Pharma Coupons. If your medication hasn't gone generic yet, ask your psychiatrist or do a quick Google search to see if there is a coupon available. You should also feel free to shop around at different pharmacies, including Walmart, Target, and Costco, for the lowest price.

Deduct Your Medical Expenses. If your insurance premium adds up to ten percent of your income, which isn't hard to pull off if you don't make a ton of money and have to buy your insurance, you may be able to write the cost off on your taxes.

Get Your Massages and Acupuncture Covered. Massage therapy, acupuncture, herbal remedies, homeopathy, and mind-body stress management are known as complementary and alternative medicine (CAM). Some insurance plans cover CAM treatments, so you'd have to make a co-pay when you see an acupuncturist or massage therapist.

Set Up a Flexible Spending Account (FSA) or a Health Savings Account (HSA). These are like savings accounts that you can only use for health care expenses. During open enrollment, you decide how much you think you'll spend on such things as therapy visits and prescription drugs in the following year. Your employer then takes that amount out of your paycheck and puts it into an FSA before your paycheck is taxed. It can be a hassle to file for reimbursements, but since you are using pre-tax dollars, a $50 co-pay is actually less. The catch is, if you don't use it, you lose it. It's a good deal if you know you're going to spend at least $100 on approved medical expenses, and are the type who can hang on to receipts. A HSA is similar to an FSA but is only for people with high-deductible insurance plans. With an HSA, you never lose the money you put in.

Use COBRA for Short-Term Coverage. It stands for the Consolidated Omnibus Budget Reconciliation Act (COBRA), but when you find out how much it costs, you might think it's a type of snake trying to poison your bank account. Under COBRA, you have the right to stay on your employer-sponsored health insurance for eighteen-to-twenty-nine months after you lose or quit your job. But, since your employer doesn't split the tab with you anymore, it is pricey. Here's a good thing to know when considering it: If you think you'll need COBRA for only a month, sign up ASAP—but don't make the first payment until the last possible minute. If you need to use health care during days one through forty-four, you will be covered as long as you pay by day forty-five. If you end up not needing to use it, just ignore that fat COBRA bill when it arrives.

Hospital Charity Care. If your income is under the federally designated poverty level, a hospital has to provide you with free or discounted "medically necessary" treatment. It usually starts with an ER visit, which can include a psych evaluation and possibly medication.

HOW REAL PEOPLE PAY FOR MENTAL HEALTH CARE

The motto for our health care system today is basically *you do you*. You choose your insurance plan, find your pros, decide what treatments you want, and deal with the bills that roll in. It's empowering—but also overwhelming. Check out what it looks like IRL for me, Shannon, Carla Jean, and Madison.

ME

I have depression and anxiety, but at this point my mental health care plan is all about maintenance. I see a psychiatrist once a year to make sure that my SSRI is still the right choice and get the prescription from my primary care doctor during my (free!) annual physical. I do see a therapist online twice a month. Right now, I'm also doing acupuncture to manage my anxiety.

What I pay:

- Employer-based PPO insurance: $313 monthly
- Online therapy session with a social worker, self-pay: $70 twice a month
- Session with a psychiatrist, co-pay: $50 once each year
- Escitalopram (Lexapro generic), co-pay: $12 monthly
- Acupuncture, sliding scale: $40 twice a month

SHANNON

Having a psychiatrist who understands my needs and prescribes the right medication for me is essential for managing my schizophrenia. I see my psychiatrist once a month and therapist every other week. I also take seven medications, although three are just "as needed." When I lived in California, my mental health care costs were insanely expensive. My medication alone was easily $1,000 each month. In NYC, I was able to qualify for Medicaid. It's the most amazing insurance I have ever had. Since I am a student with no income, I don't have to pay a premium to get benefits.

What I Pay:

- Medicaid insurance: $0
- Session with a psychiatrist, self-pay: $250 monthly
- Medications: $0-$4 each, monthly
- Session with in-network therapist: $0

CARLA JEAN

Yoga and spending time outdoors in natural light are as important for dealing with my depression and seasonal affective disorder as therapy and medication. I also use a light therapy lamp when I'm starting to feel down during the dark winter months. My therapist doesn't accept my insurance, so I pay out-of-pocket, which is doable right now because I am only going as needed, usually less than once each month.

What I Pay:

- Employer-based insurance: $120 monthly
- Session with a therapist, self-pay: $80

- Sertraline (Zoloft generic), co-pay: $13 monthly
- Yoga class: $15 per class, twice a month
- Light therapy lamp: $100
- Hiking and walking in natural light, weekly: $0

MADISON

I no longer see a therapist or psychiatrist to help deal with my depression *because* of the cost. I'm insured through my employer and was given the opportunity to attend five free sessions with a therapist through the employee assistance program (EAP).

What I Pay:

- Employer-based insurance: $70 monthly
- Five sessions with a therapist via EAP: $0
- Celexa, co-pay: $7 monthly

PART FOUR

BE KIND TO YOUR BODY

When you are struggling with mental illness, it can be easy to forget the rest of your body. You may even be hurting yourself on purpose to make your outside match how you feel inside.

Taking care of your physical health will improve your mental health while treating your body like shit will make it worse. You don't have to become a health junkie—you can start by making small changes. Over time, they will make a big difference.

Fitness pro Bill Phillips once said, "Food is the most widely abused anti-anxiety drug in America, and exercise is the most potent yet underutilized antidepressant."

This part of the book explains all of the little actions you can take to stay mentally healthy every day.

DON'T EAT JUNK

True story: I once had dinner with a woman who told me that my brother's schizophrenia could be cured with an all vegan diet. I wanted to reach across the table and stab her with my butter knife. Instead, I politely said, "Hmm. That's interesting," and spent the rest of the dinner fuming. Was she seriously saying that the illness that was destroying my brother's life and causing us so much pain would disappear if he switched from chicken quesadillas to bean burritos?

There isn't a perfect meal plan that will instantly melt away all of your symptoms. But researchers have learned a lot about what food does to your brain, and their studies have shown that some foods can help reduce symptoms, while others can make them worse.

Your mission is to incorporate as many of those symptom-fighting foods as possible into what you already eat. You should also try to eat three meals a day, definitely don't skip breakfast, and consume at least the minimum number of calories your body needs. (In general, women who are moderately active need 2,000 calories a day and men need 2,500.)

GOOD VS. BAD MOOD FOOD

The dirty truth about comfort foods is that they only make you feel good while you are eating them. Once you've digested, they won't do anything for your mood.

No surprise here: Good mood foods include whole grains, leafy greens, and lean protein—basically, the kinds of food you know you should be eating anyway. If like me, you have trouble staying motivated to eat healthily, maybe it'll help to know that choosing chicken salad over a cheeseburger and fries won't just help you fit into your skinny jeans. It can make you feel less depressed and anxious, too.

Good Mood Foods

Start small by working these ten foods into your diet. When you are ready for more, check out the Mediterranean diet, which is made up of healthy foods proven to prevent depression.

1. Fruits
2. Leafy green veggies such as spinach, broccoli, and kale
3. Whole-grain bread and pasta
4. Fish—especially salmon, trout, mackerel, and tuna
5. Nuts
6. Olive oil
7. Milk
8. Orange juice
9. Whole-grain cereals enriched with vitamin D
10. Eight glasses of water a day

BAD MOOD FOODS

These foods can still make special appearances from time to time, but start to eliminate them from your everyday diet. It might be easier if you cut out one each week until you are comfortable with the process.

1. Caffeine, especially in sugary sodas
2. Fried foods (Sorry, french fries)
3. Ice cream
4. Processed foods such as chips and crackers
5. Candy and sugary sweets

✱ REAL TALK:

63% of people surveyed believe that what they eat impacts their mental health.

MOVE YOUR BODY

Practically every trainer alive says that that best exercise for you is the one you'll stick with. Whether you suit up and go for a run outside or get your cardio while mindlessly watching reality TV on the elliptical, you're burning calories. If your goals are strictly physical, it makes no difference how you burn those calories.

Working out for your mental health is different. While some exercise is still better than nothing, your goal should be to get sweaty enough for the endorphins to kick in and send a "Hey, this is awesome!" message to your brain.

Vigorous exercise releases endorphins, and, as Elle Woods so aptly put it in *Legally Blonde*, "Endorphins make you happy." Studies that associate physical activity with mental wellness are piling up and some researchers believe that exercise can be as effective for depression as therapy or medication. You need thirty minutes three to five times each week to get the mental benefits of exercise.

✱ REAL TALK:

Best exercises for mental health, according to survey respondents.

1. Yoga

2. Running

3. Dance

4. Using cardio equipment at the gym

5. Cycling or spinning

6. Swimming

7. Lifting weights

8. Boxing

9. Martial arts

10. CrossFit

GET ENOUGH SLEEP

Sleep is a superpower. It resets your body, boosts your mood, lowers your stress level, helps you stay focused during your awake hours, ups your sex drive, helps manage weight, keeps your immune system and memory strong, and adds years to your life by helping ward off killer diseases. Adults need between seven and nine hours each night to recharge, while teens need even more: between nine and ten hours.

That's why it is so damn frustrating when you can't fall or stay asleep. Not only does sleep deprivation rob you of the benefits of sleep, but it also increases your negative thoughts and messes with your ability to cope.

It's no coincidence that sleep issues make the list of symptoms for almost all of the mental disorders discussed in this book. Having trouble with sleep is one way your body is telling you that something is wrong. If you are often tired, fall asleep watching TV, or feel like you need an IV drip of caffeine to get through the day, you probably aren't getting enough sleep. These tips should help you get more ZZZs naturally.

- Give yourself a bedtime that is at least eight hours before your typical wake-up call. Bonus points if you give yourself a half hour to an hour to wind down even before that. Put away your cell (hello, airplane mode) and take a bath, play soft music, meditate, stretch, or whatever works to quiet your mind and relax your body.

- Cut back on the caffeine. Swapping coffee for green tea is always a healthy move, but if you must have your java, consider lattes, which typically have much less caffeine. If you haven't already cut out soda, switch to the caffeine-free kind. Consider implementing a "No caffeine after noon" rule.

- Make your bed a cozy place. If you can, invest in a comfortable mattress and bed linens that make you want to spend some QT under the covers. At the very least, make your bed. There's something so soothing about crawling into a bed that has been made up, especially with clean sheets.

If you have trouble sleeping more than three nights a week for a month, it's time to chat with your therapist or primary care doctor. It doesn't automatically mean you need sleep medication.

Cognitive behavior therapy (CBT), which I mentioned in part two, works well for insomnia, and mindfulness exercises such as meditation and deep breathing can help you deal with anxiety and the thoughts that may be keeping you awake. There's also chance your sleep problems could have a physical cause, such as a thyroid problem or sleep apnea.

GO TO THE DOCTOR

People with a serious mental illness such as bipolar disorder or schizophrenia have a shorter life expectancy than everyone else—by ten-to-twenty years! And guess what? It isn't because of suicide. It's because, for a long time, people with mental disorders smoked too much, rarely went to the doctor, and didn't follow through on their doctors' advice when they did. Add to that the fact that many of the old-school antipsychotic medications made people gain weight. It was all a perfect storm for causing cancer, heart disease, and diabetes. I'm using the past tense because this needs to be over. Here's how *not* to be a statistic:

- Find a primary care doctor and go in for a physical. Your doctor should take your blood pressure, listen to your heart and breathing, do blood work, and perform any other tests recommended for your age group. Women should get pap smears at least once every three years. If you've had sex with someone new since your last exam, get an STD test.

- Mark the date of your physical on your calendar and make an appointment for about the same time every year.

- Get all the immunizations and vaccines that you can. Most people need the Tdap, Meningococcal, Pneumococcal, MMR, HPV, Chickenpox, Hepatitis A and C, and Hib.

- At the exam, tell your doctor about your mental disorder and the medications that you take. Also tell her about any issues you are having with sleep, weight, or pain. If you feel like she isn't listening to you, find another doctor. Some symptoms of mental illness—such as chest pain, headaches, and fatigue—can be confused with a physical illness. It's not your job to figure that out. You aren't the one that went to medical school.

- Get a flu shot every fall, even if you never get sick. Shots are offered at lots of pharmacies and are covered by most insurance plans. The more people who get flu shots, the less flu there is going around. Some people can't take it and could get really sick if they got the flu. Do it for them.

- Take a multi-vitamin. (Adults can take Flintstones vitamins, too!)

- Even if your goal isn't to have pearly whites à la Joe Biden, you do need to go to the dentist once each year to prevent gum disease and tooth loss.

- Don't smoke, use drugs, or binge drink.

- Remember that you are in charge of your mind and your body.

DITCH YOUR VICES

At the risk of sounding like Nancy Reagan (the First Lady who told everyone to "Just say no" to drugs), this is the part of the book where I tell you that drugs are bad for you—but maybe for different reasons than you've heard before.

Cigarettes

I don't have to tell you that cigarettes are evil. You've seen the commercials where people talk out of a machine hooked up to a hole in their neck, or wear a little bag where their lungs used to be. For some reason, even though everyone knows that cigarettes can kill you, people still smoke—especially people with mental illness. In fact, forty percent of all cigarettes are sold to people with mental illness. Why? For one thing, smoking relieves stress. It makes you feel calm. And when you are struggling with the pain of depression, who cares about the risks of smoking a cigarette?

Honestly, it seems unfair to take away one of the few things that can make a person feel better. If that's you, please consider cutting back. And then hopefully you can cut back some more when you are feeling better. If the idea of going cold turkey, or even cutting back, is overwhelming, try nicotine gum, a patch, or even hypnosis. You can get help quitting with a free smoking cessation program at www.Smokefree.gov. And, if you don't smoke, don't start.

BOOZE

Confession: One of the reasons I was reluctant to start taking antidepressants was that I was afraid I'd have to give up alcohol. Drinking was a big part of my life back then. I never thought I was an alcoholic because it didn't control my life, but at times, it was absolutely the center of it. I loved my boozy brunches, work happy hours, wine-fueled dinner parties, and tipsy first dates. Thank god a friend told me that you could drink when you're on an SSRI! (And really, did I think that the thirteen percent of Americans who take antidepressants are all teetotalers?) What she didn't tell me was that it would permanently lower my tolerance for alcohol. I learned *that* lesson by getting too drunk and embarrassing myself.

If you usually drink several nights a week, the Center for Disease Control's recommendations may seem like a prank. They recommend that women have no more than one drink a day, and men have only two. If that sounds unrealistic, start by drinking less each time you go out, and cutting back on the number of days per week you drink. Easier said than done, I know, but drinking in moderation *feels better* than overdoing it, once you get used to it.

POT

If your grandma can smoke weed for her glaucoma, and it's legal for medical use in twenty-nine states and counting, how bad can it be? Answer: Not that bad for most people. Marijuana has enough positive benefits that in some states it is prescribed for people with anxiety and PTSD. But, those benefits don't translate for all mental disorders. In fact, there is a lot of evidence that MJ can trigger psychosis (a symptom of schizophrenia, schizoaffective disorder, bipolar disorder, or major depression that makes you lose touch with reality) in people who are already at risk for it.

Only eight to eleven percent of people who use marijuana get addicted, but since even your grandma is smoking pot these days, that's a lot of people. The reason weed is often labeled as a gateway drug is that almost everyone who does harder drugs starts out with pot. That doesn't mean that one minute you are sharing a joint at a party and the next you are in an alley with a needle in your arm. But pot does tend to lower people's inhibitions, so they are more willing to try other drugs. If addiction is an issue in your family or you are at risk for psychosis, it's not worth it.

So, what about synthetic marijuana, often known as K2, Spice, or fake weed? This stuff is made from herbs (but not that herb) and then sprayed with chemicals that mimic THC. Because it's still relatively new, some varieties are legal and aren't detectable in most urine tests. But, unlike real pot, synthetic marijuana has been known to make people violent, suicidal, and psychotic—and not just people who have a mental disorder. Plus, fake pot is often mixed with other drugs and toxic chemicals, so deadly overdoses can happen and are becoming more common.

PRESCRIPTION PAINKILLERS AND HEROIN (AKA OPIOIDS)

The only time you should ever take painkillers is when you are really, really in pain and your doctor has prescribed them for you. Then, take them as directed, and don't ask for a refill. Otherwise, *forget it.*

If this sounds harsh, it's because about half of the people who end up using heroin (the worst of the worst) started with pills. Right now, there is a drug called fentanyl in the heroin supply that is ten times more lethal than straight-up heroin. That means you are more likely to OD and die than ever before. In 2016, 42,000 people died from an opiate overdose. That's the highest death toll during a single year of any drug epidemic ever.

UPPERS: STIMULANTS AND AMPHETAMINES

Uppers—known as molly, ecstasy, coke, MDMA, speed, ICE, and meth—are designed to give you a temporary high and SO MUCH ENERGY that you feel invincible, sexually charged, and super alert. But what goes up must come down. Almost all of these drugs end up making you severely depressed as soon as the high wears off. It's a real bummer for everyone, but it's dangerous for those of us who already feel that way. These drugs can also cause panic attacks (the thing that feels like a heart attack), hallucinations, delusions, or make you paranoid or anxious. And that's just what they can do to your mental health. Other "not worth it" side effects include a reduced sex drive, gastrointestinal problems, heart disease, seizures, and stroke.

PSYCHEDELICS (LSD/ACID, MESCALINE, MUSHROOMS, IBOGAINE)

Psychedelics such as magic mushrooms, acid, and mescaline are known for their mind-altering highs. They change your sense of perception, often making you hallucinate. Some researchers are looking into the positive effects that microdoses of psychedelic drugs may have on people with PTSD. A few years from now, you might be given a tiny pill with a little LSD inside during your therapy session. Even that won't be the same as heading out to the dessert with some mescaline. For now, it's best to stay away from drugs designed to alter your perceptions.

SELF CARE IS ...

WROTE DOWN MY FEELINGS

HAD ENOUGH WATER

WENT OUTSIDE

SANG MY HEART OUT!

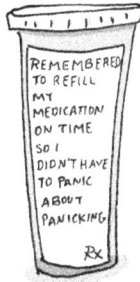
REMEMBERED TO REFILL MY MEDICATION ON TIME SO I DIDN'T HAVE TO PANIC ABOUT PANICKING
Rx

EXERCISED 1ST EVEN WHEN I DIDN'T WANT TO

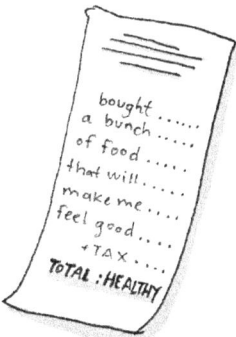
bought a bunch of food that will make me feel good + TAX
TOTAL : HEALTHY

Allowed myself time to recover

vocalized MY NEEDS

PRACTICE LEGIT SELF-CARE

Self-care started off as a term used by doctors and nurses to describe patients with chronic illnesses who they felt could take care of themselves at home instead of staying in the hospital. Today, it's a buzz phrase that has launched a $10 billion industry. Type the term into Google, and you'll find that *self-care* has been applied to everything from driving with the windows down to painting your nails.

The self-care as I want to talk about it is not getting a mani/pedi, haircut, or wax. That's not self-care. It's grooming. I believe that self-care is taking care of yourself with the goal of managing your stress and emotions. It is the things you do to help prevent flare-ups of your illness (kind of how flossing helps prevent cavities).

Here's a list of cheap, easy, and effective self-care activities that are worth working into your life.

1. Meditate
2. Take a walk, ideally in nature
3. Listen to or play music
4. Read novels
5. Keep a journal
6. Soak in a hot bath
7. Practice deep breathing
8. Cuddle up with a pet (even if you have to borrow one for the day)
9. Take a nap

10. Get acupuncture

11. Bake a sweet treat for yourself or someone else

12. Draw, color, or paint

13. Work on a puzzle

14. Pray

15. Make a gratitude list

16. Spend ten minutes in the sun

17. Recite positive affirmations

18. Have a massage

19. Get a plant or fresh flowers

20. Drink tea and just be still

HOW TO DEAL WITH THE TERRIBLE NEWS WE HEAR EVERY DAY

Breaking news always gives me a rush, but when the story is horrific, as it so often is these days, it can take a toll on mental health. Research has proven a link between a barrage of bad news and anxiety, depression, and substance use disorder. Staying on top of current events is a priority for me, but it isn't worth risking my mental health.

Now, when I get a BREAKING NEWS! alert about something more important than a high-profile celebrity breakup, I follow these rules:

- **Decide What You Need to Know.** If there is a terrorist attack or natural disaster in your area, you need to know how to stay safe. You also need to know what, if anything, you can do to help. Everything else, from reading how a bomb was made to seeing pictures of people running through the streets with their hair on fire, isn't critical information.

- **Stick to the Facts.** There is often very little actual news following a BREAKING NEWS! alert. When possible, as in, when the action is happening far away from you and your loved ones, try to wait a day or two for all of the facts to come together before you delve deeper into the story. That way, you won't become anxious over rumors and speculation, which is all the commentators know in the immediate aftermath.

- **Set Limits.** It's helpful to remember that until very recently, people got most of their information from their morning paper and evening newscast. Now, horrible news comes at you from all directions, so it's best to set limits on the number of times each day you check your preferred news sources. And you might consider avoiding social media altogether, at least until the smoke clears.

PART FIVE

RELATIONSHIPS MATTER

Every relationship, from your true love to the person you sit next to at the office, can impact your mental health. Some of these people will lift you up, support you, and bring you so much joy. Others will bring you down, and maybe kick you while you're there.

Your mental health can also affect your relationships. My second episode with depression, the one after my brother went missing, changed virtually all of mine. It manifested as anger towards myself, and everyone around me, especially my family. His downfall broke me, and I couldn't imagine that our mother or sister would ever understand the deepness of that pain. Instead of trying to comfort each other, I retreated, putting up walls to cement the physical and emotional distance between us.

Some of my friends didn't know how to relate to me, and I didn't know how to accept the support from those who tried. I have very fuzzy memories of that time, but I do remember that when a few co-workers invited me to take a day trip and go kayaking, I barely spoke a word to them the whole day. They were trying to connect and I should have opened up, but I didn't think I mattered enough.

My best friend, who was also my roommate, was falling in love with the guy who would eventually become her husband. I was super jealous that she was happy and couldn't devote all of her attention to me. I didn't realize that at the time. I was too busy throwing shade at her in the moments when I wasn't curled up in my bed. Thankfully, she understood I was just in a very dark place and forgave me for being a total bitch when I eventually apologized.

Instead of connecting with people who were trying to reach out, I put more effort than I should have into my toxic relationships. Of course, that's not how I thought of them at the time. Since then, I've learned that some people are drawn to those who seem broken because it makes them feel better by comparison. They thrive on your pain because it lessens their own. I eventually ended those friendships, and though I miss some things about them, I know I am better off.

One of those relationships was with a guy who I wasn't that into at first. I was tired of feeling alone, so I molded myself into the girlfriend I thought he wanted. I figured this was as good as it was going to get. When he eventually broke up with me, I was devastated, not so much because I missed him, but because my plan had not worked. Now, I was alone again.

At that point, I had begun working at the National Suicide Prevention Lifeline. There I met three badass women who would become my lifeline, and me theirs. At our core, we each want to make the best out of our very imperfect lives and help others do the same—and that's what our friendship is based on.

Not everyone thought working in suicide prevention was so cool. I watched many a date become uncomfortable when I mentioned my work. It was a deal breaker for some, but I had no patience for a guy, or anyone, who couldn't get on board with my new life's mission. When I told my now-husband, Barry, where I worked on our first date, he said, "Oh cool, I used to volunteer there." That tipped me off that he would be supportive not only of my work but my mental health as well.

At the end of the four years that I spent dealing with my brother's illness, having an episode of depression, and eventually rebuilding my life, the people I spent my time with had changed. I would love to have friendships that date back to the playground, but I didn't meet most of my people until my thirties. That's OK.

I've learned some hard lessons about who you should, and shouldn't, let into your life. I want to help you sort the people who can build you up when you are struggling, from those who are just bringing you down. For every person who sucks, there are so many more who make you feel loved and will have your back when you need them. Your mission is to find those people and be as kind to them as they are to you.

PEOPLE YOU NEED IN YOUR LIFE

Even if you have thousands of followers on social media, most of us can count the number of people who we are close to on one hand. They can be anyone from your mom, aunt, brother by another mother, sorority sister, boyfriend, or brand new friend you've bonded with. That doesn't mean you should dump everyone else. Far from it.

Think of your relationships as a collection of circles. In one circle you have the people who will have your back no matter what. We'll call them your A-List. Your B-List circle is made up of family and friends you like spending time with and who make you feel good about yourself, and your C-List is filled with casual friends who usually serve a singular purpose in your life.

A-List. These are your BFFs, close family, and your SO who you spend the majority of your time with. They are people you trust and want to help you deal with whatever life throws your way. It's a good idea to let your A-List crew know all about your mental disorder, how you are managing it, and what some of your triggers are. As the people who know you best, they can help you identify when you are starting to experience more symptoms. They are also the ones who will keep showing up for you even when you are trying hard to push everyone away.

Some of us go into isolation mode when we are really hurting, and don't always give our friends and family the chance to be supportive. It can be awkward or embarrassing when someone has seen you at your lowest point. You don't have to let everyone in, but you should allow your A-List be there for you. And you should be there for them.

B-List. These are people you share a bond with and feel good being around. It includes your new-ish boyfriend or girlfriend, your group chat, and the rest of your family. Since you don't share your deepest thoughts and feelings with this group, it's not necessary to fill them in on everything your therapist says. If you decide not to tell your B-List about your mental disorder, you can still enlist them in your self-care and healthy activities.

C-List. This is the group who hang out in one area of your life. Think co-workers, teammates, relatives you don't see often, or someone you are dating very casually. When you are around them, you usually keep the convo light and airy—and mostly about school, work, family, soccer or whatever ties you together. They don't need to know everything about you, so you don't have to tell them about your mental illness unless you are comfortable.

Keep in mind that these circles are always changing. Some people may start off as C-List friends and eventually become your A-List.

WHAT'S THE DEAL WITH PEER SUPPORT?

Peer-to-peer is the clinical term for friendship between two people who have been through similar things. (I told you mental health pros have their own language!)

It's when you can count on people who are dealing with the same issues. Kind of like having a gym buddy. You can usually find them at a support group. A peer will probably ask you lots of questions about how you are feeling and will encourage you to stay focused on your recovery. Here's a list of what you can expect from a good peer. It doubles as a list of things that make you one as well.

- Talk/text/chat regularly
- Know when to encourage your friend to see a professional
- Encourage healthy activities like exercise and proper nutrition
- Help them stay on top of their treatment routine
- Be sensitive to their feelings
- Know that you have limits to how much you can help

DEALING WITH HATERS AND OTHER PEOPLE WHO AREN'T GOOD FOR YOU

Lots of people in this world suck. Some of them may even be in your family. Just because you are related to someone, or grew up together, doesn't mean that they have earned lifetime status in your circles. You can't really kick someone off of your family tree, but you can decide what kind of relationship you will have with them. But first, you have to know who they are.

HOW TO SPOT THEM

Haters. Haters are people who, despite all the science and evidence to the contrary, don't think that mental illness is a real thing. They wish you'd snap out of it and pull yourself up by your bootstraps. It's hard to deal with the haters when you are hurting, but it can't always be avoided. They aren't necessarily bad people. They just don't mesh with who you are and what you need in your life right now.

Toxics. Toxic relationships make you feel bad about yourself, which is one reason they are harder to spot when you are struggling. It's easy to tell when a person is passive-aggressive or jealous, but some of the other signs, like being secretive or avoiding you, are trickier to spot if you are already feeling low and isolating yourself. Think of it this way, if interacting with a certain person always makes you feel more anxious or depressed, you are probably in a toxic relationship. It is possible to improve your relationship if you are willing to be honest about the way you feel and both agree to work on treating each other better. But, if you realize the person you have a toxic relationship with has one with *everyone* in their life, you're better off moving on.

Abusers. One of the lessons from the barrage of recent abuse scandals is that it takes many different shapes. Most forms of abuse are an attempt to control someone—whether it is physically, sexually, or emotionally. If you are experiencing abuse of any kind from anyone, it's important to get help immediately. The longer you are in an abusive relationship, the harder it may be to end it, and the more dangerous it can become.

HOW TO DEAL WITH THEM

There's no need to go through a big dramatic breakup with the people who you don't want to keep in your life. You could ghost them, but it isn't very nice, especially since they are probably hurting or dealing with their own issues as well. It may be easier on both of you emotionally if you let the relationships fade over time.

You can gradually distance yourself from someone who isn't good for you by setting clear boundaries. For example, maybe you would rather not spend any more one-on-one time together but are fine hanging out as a group. If that feels like too much to you, take it down a notch. Therapists are super helpful with boundary-setting.

You may need to be direct with someone about why you don't want to spend as much time with them. Although it won't be easy, it can be as simple as saying, "I don't feel good about myself when we are together," or "It hurts me that you downplay what I am dealing with emotionally."

One exception: If someone is threatening you or physically abusing you, your boundaries need to be firm, maybe even in the form of a restraining order.

WHEN TO TELL A DATE YOUR MENTAL ILLNESS

Nothing kills the vibe of a first date faster than saying "My psychiatrist says..." This timeline will help you figure out the right time to unload.

First Date. Nope.

Second Date. Start slow. You can get a sense of how she will react by name-dropping a mental health charity you are thinking of volunteering for or bringing up the latest celeb to announce they have a disorder. Another idea is to bring up a "friend" who just happens to be in the exact situation you are in. If you get the sense that she's is open to it, or is also one of the millions of people who deal with a mental disorder, go ahead and mention it. Just don't assume that it was the deal-breaker if date two doesn't turn into a third. There's no point wasting your precious time trying to figure out the many unsolved mysteries of the dating world.

First Two Months of Dating. After three to five dates, you should be able to share some truths about yourself. One way to bring it up is to be direct and say something like, "I have bipolar disorder, and I manage it by seeing a therapist and taking medication." Try not to give it more weight than you would when mentioning a physical illness like asthma or diabetes. Yes, it's a big deal, but it's not something you should be ashamed of.

Within Six Months of Dating. It's a bit much to expect that your new girlfriend will become an advocate warrior for mental health, but she should at least know taking care of your mind and body is an essential part of your life. At this point in your relationship, if you haven't shared your experience and find yourself hiding your medication or lying about your therapy appointments, she might not be the right match for you.

REAL TALK:
40% of percent of people surveyed said their mental health was a factor in a break-up.

HOW TO MAKE A BREAKUP SUCK LESS

Ending a relationship with someone (even if it was your idea) can trigger symptoms of sadness, hopelessness, and anxiety. A breakup may sting like a death in the family—except that the person you thought you couldn't live without is alive and well, possibly banging someone else.

Don't give your breakup that power. Put down the Ben & Jerry's and turn off Adele. Like it or not, you have to get moving to move on. Consider this your game plan for getting from the minute your heart was stomped on to the day when you barely think about it at all.

Get out of bed. Give yourself a bedtime and set an alarm to wake up at a decent hour, even on the weekend. Your bed is for sleeping, not wallowing. There's no one to see there anyway. (Sorry.)

Ghost your ex. Decide how long you can realistically handle not talking/texting/chatting your ex. This is a stretch goal, so think big, but if you work together or have to be around each other for a legit reason, it's not realistic to be MIA forever. Try to give yourself one or two solid weeks to deal with the hurt and pain before you have to see your ex's face again.

Don't stalk. It's tempting to analyze your ex's every tweet, insta, and post. But trying to decode what every dumb GIF means is an anxiety-provoking waste of energy.

Get a giant tattoo on your back. Just kidding, definitely don't do that unless it was already scheduled. You're going to want to wait a few months before making any decisions that you'll have to live with your entire life.

Lean on your friends. Hopefully, your A-List has already checked in on you, but when shit happens, some people tend to lie low. That doesn't mean they don't want to be there for you; they just don't know how. Tell them what you need, and everyone wins. Don't stop with your closest friends. This is an all-hands meeting and everyone, from your drinking buddies to office friends, can do something to help you take your mind off your broken heart.

Pack your schedule. Join a rec sports team, take some night classes, and book lunches and drinks with people you've been meaning to catch-up with. You probably don't feel like it, but do it anyway. It's not about how you feel right now. It's how you will feel after you've spent your a newly single weeks getting back out there and participating in (slowly, but surely) your life.

Write it all down. You can start with an e-mail detailing all of the ways your ex stomped on your heart. Just don't send it. In fact, you don't even have to save it.

Talk to a therapist. If you're feeling sad, hopeless, or having symptoms of depression after a couple of weeks, it›s a good idea to call in a pro. They can help you with the loss and figure out if there are other factors at play. For example, it could be that the breakup of your college relationship is also making you anxious about the next stage of your life.

PART SIX

FIND YOUR PURPOSE

Let me introduce you to one of my heroes, Elyn Saks. When she was eight, she started having symptoms of schizophrenia. She had her first psychotic break while studying at Oxford. Her delusions made her believe that she had killed hundreds of thousands of people with her mind. Once, she had a hallucination that a man was standing over her with a raised knife. She was hospitalized again during her time at Yale Law School. By her count, she's logged hundreds of days in psychiatric hospitals.

Elyn still managed to get a law degree *and* earn a Ph.D. in psychoanalytic science. She was awarded the MacArthur "Genius Grant" (fellow awardees include *Hamilton* creator Lin-Manuel Miranda and author David Foster Wallace) and used the prize money to create the Saks Institute for Mental Health Law, Policy, and Ethics at the University of Southern California. On top of that, she is happily married and about as famous as a mental health lawyer can be.

Your mental health has nothing to do with your intelligence level or creativity. It doesn't mean you are smarter and it doesn't mean you are dumber. Whether you are destined for a law degree or feel satisfied with a high school diploma, your mental disorder should not limit you. In fact, there are laws on the books and support out there to make sure that you have every opportunity that you need to be successful.

Allow me to explain how you can navigate school and work so that you can make your dreams happen. Since, for some of us, fulfillment isn't easily found in the classroom or at a job, there's also information about how you can get involved with an organization you care about.

MANAGE YOUR MENTAL HEALTH ON CAMPUS

Mental illness often rears its ugly head just before you finish high school or after you've gone off to college—as if those years weren't challenging enough. One-in-five students deals with a mental health issue while in college.

Most universities have put two and two together and started to offer extra resources and created policies to help students who are struggling. Plus, mental disorders are considered disabilities and are covered under the Rehabilitation Act and Americans with Disabilities Act, which require schools to provide equal benefits, services, and opportunities. It's not like grading on a curve; it means that they will provide "reasonable accommodations" to give you a fair shot at succeeding in school. These laws apply to public schools and private ones that receive federal funding.

✳ REAL TALK:
More than half of people surveyed said their mental health impacted their GPA.

ACCOMMODATIONS THAT WILL MAKE YOUR LIFE EASIER

If you want to take advantage of these accommodations, and there's no reason not to, you have to let your school's office of accessibilities know that you have a disability. In some cases,

EVERYTHING IS GOING TO BE OK

you have to do this at the beginning of each semester. You will probably need your therapist to sign off on an official form, and she may need to go into detail about why you need each accommodation.

Not to worry: Your university is not going to stamp your diagnosis on your forehead. They are responsible for keeping your health records confidential. You may need to talk to your professors to let them know you need a particular accommodation, but you don't have to go into detail about why.

Here's what you can expect your school to do:

- Let you register for classes early so you can create a schedule that works best for you
- Grant early access to a class syllabus and textbooks
- Allow you to take breaks during long lectures
- Let you use an audio recorder (most professors will let anyone do this)
- Give you more time on exams or let you take a test in a private room
- Allow you to take exams in a different format, such as writing an essay instead of a multiple choice test
- Give you an extension on add/drop dates
- Allow you to take a lighter course load

HOW TO TAKE A MEDICAL LEAVE OF ABSENCE

If you are hospitalized or struggling to keep up with your classes while dealing with symptoms of mental illness, you may need to take a break from school. It is completely legit to put academics on the backburner and put your mental health first.

But, don't just stop showing up. You can apply to take a "leave of absence" for a semester or a few years. You'll get incompletes in your classes (way better than Fs) and may be able to apply your tuition towards another semester. Depending on your school, it may be called a "leave of absence," "medical leave of absence," or "emergency leave." It's designed to let you take time to focus on your health so that you can eventually return and be successful in school.

Like everything related to academia, this will involve paperwork and deadlines. It may be the last thing on your mind, but you need to contact your advisor or the Dean of Students to take an official leave. You'll want to ask about specific requirements and documentation, how a leave might impact your financial aid, and how to re-enroll. If it's too much for you to take on, enlist a friend or family member to help with the logistics.

Although it's a tough decision, many people I interviewed in this book say that taking a leave of absence was critical to their recovery. If you need to do it, make sure you have a plan in place to continue or accelerate your treatment, a supportive place to live, and a realistic idea of when you will go back.

Leaves of absence aren't for everyone. I was a junior in college when I had my first episode of depression. Although I hadn't yet been diagnosed, I knew that leaving school would make my mental health worse. At the time, I could only get health insurance from my university and didn't have anywhere else to go. Plus, even though I was struggling and my grades were not stellar, I was very involved with my college newspaper. The promise of fresh news cycle got me out of bed each morning, and I relied on the support of my newspaper friends. Leaving school would have been giving up the footing that I did have, even if it wasn't stable.

✳ REAL TALK:

30% of people surveyed took at least one semester off to deal with their mental health.

TRANSITION BACK-TO-SCHOOL WHEN YOU'RE READY

If you do take a leave of absence, these tips will help you when you are back on campus.

- **Stay in touch.** It's a good idea to stay connected to at least one friend who is on campus. You don't have to let her know everything that is happening with you, but it will be much easier to go back knowing that you'll see a friendly face.

- **Keep your advisor in the loop.** Find time to send your advisor a quick e-mail each semester you are away, letting him know that you still plan to re-enroll. When you are back, prepare to meet up to go over your program requirements so you can stay on track to graduate.

- **Plan ahead.** Remember that long period in between when you applied to college and started classes? That hasn't changed. During your absence, keep your eye on application and registration deadlines, so you aren't stuck waiting an extra semester for classes to start.

- **Pace yourself.** You may want to start back part-time or take some of the "easier" courses during your first semester back. Try not to think about catching up. It's more important to learn to balance school and life while taking care of your mental health.

- **Be patient.** You may be a year or more behind the class-mates you met as a freshman. It will be frustrating to watch them graduate before you, but very soon when you are all living the post-college life, those years won't matter at all.

DEAL WITH MENTAL ILLNESS AT THE OFFICE

Dealing with a mental health issue can make the daily grind that much harder. Thanks to disability laws and the work of advocacy organizations, many employers now recognize that it is good business to create a mentally healthy environment.

That means treating their staff—you!—with respect and acknowledging that mental health is as important as physical health. They provide accommodations (see below) not just to people with mental disorders, but to all employees. In addition to offering mental health benefits as part of an insurance package, they also have an employee assistance program, which provides free, confidential support and a handful of free therapy visits.

Of course, not all employers or bosses are on board. It's on you to know your rights and request the accommodations you may need. You should figure out what type of employment works best for you, and learn when you need to take time off (whether it's one day or three months) to focus on your mental health.

KNOW YOUR RIGHTS

It's straight-up illegal for your employer to discriminate against you because of your mental illness. That means your boss can't fire you or deny you a promotion just because you have a mental disorder. It's also against the law, per the Americans with Disabilities Act, to harass you because of your disorder or force you to take a leave of absence.

You do have to be able to show up for work and do your job, but the law requires employers to make "reasonable accommodations" so that you can. It's reasonable to ask your boss to adjust your hours so you can make your weekly therapy appointment. It's not reasonable to request that your workload be dramatically reduced to minimize stress. FYI, you may need a note from your therapist that explains why the accommodations are necessary.

Here's what your employer is required to do for you:

- Allow you to use a noise canceling headset or sound machine to reduce distractions
- Give you uninterrupted time to get work done
- Make it possible for you to get sunlight exposure, either by taking breaks outside or bringing in a light therapy lamp
- Allow you to take time off for appointments
- Create a flexible work environment with a modified break schedule and possibly the opportunity to work from home on pre-determined days
- Provide you with both written and verbal instructions for project and task assignments
- Grant permission to record meetings or trainings
- Schedule weekly meetings to discuss your workload
- Allow you to bring a support animal to work
- Provide a quiet and private space for you to take breaks to practice relaxation techniques

HOW TO GET $$ IF YOU REALLY CAN'T WORK

Social Security is most commonly known as an allowance for seniors, but if your mental illness makes it hard for you to keep a job, you may be able to qualify no matter how old you are.

There are two different types of Social Security. One is Social Security Income (known as SSI). The other, Social Security Disability Insurance (SSDI), is a program for people who worked for several years and paid into Social Security. It gets automatically taken out of your paycheck if you're employed "on the books." If your illness started before your twenty-second birthday, you might be able to qualify for SSDI under your parents.

Both SSI and SSDI are programs run by the Social Security Administration for people who cannot work because of a chronic or fatal illness. Most of the disorders covered in this book—depression, anxiety, panic disorder, PTSD, OCD, bipolar disorder, schizophrenia, and eating disorders—are on that list.

Having a diagnosis isn't enough to collect a check. A doctor or psychiatrist must verify that you have several symptoms that limit your ability to hold down a job. Typically, you must have had that illness for at least one year and aren't able to adjust to a new work situation because of your symptoms. For example, you might qualify if you have depression and are currently dealing with at least five symptoms and have difficulty understanding basic information, interacting with others, and trouble concentrating or managing yourself.

You must be between ages eighteen and sixty-five, never married, and a US citizen. Plus, you need to be unemployed or making less than $1,180 each month.

Here's the catch: In 2018, the monthly payment for SSI is $750/month. Most states add on a state supplementary between $10-200/month. It's better than nothing, but it's tough to live on $750 each month.

To apply, use the online form at www.Socialsecurity.gov/ap-plyforbenefits or call 800-772-1213. You have to apply for SSI and SSID and other government benefits like Medicaid and SNAP (aka, food stamps) at the same time. Expect to hand over medical records and information about your employment history and education.

FIND A JOB THAT WORKS FOR YOU

Working sixty-hour weeks isn't good for anyone's mental health. That "all work and no play" lifestyle won't just make Jack a dull boy—it'll invite his symptoms to make a comeback. Balancing work and life is hard, but it almost always starts with choosing a job that allows you to have enough time to take care of your relationships and your mental and physical health.

Some people need a lot of time to manage their mental illness. That's totally OK. In fact, there are plenty of alternatives to traditional full-time employment.

Part-Time Work. Having a part-time job doesn't mean working retail or serving coffee. More than twenty-eight million people in the US work part-time, in almost every single sector. These jobs offer more flexibility so that you can stay on top of your treatment and self-care routine. Plus, if you work more than thirty hours per week, your employer is required to offer health insurance.

Temporary or Freelance Employment. "Temping" is a great way to build your resume and earn some cash if you don't feel you can commit to a full-time job. You will typically work the standard thirty-five to forty hours a week, but probably won't be able to take advantage of the company's health plan or other benefits. In return, you'll have the freedom to take time off whenever you need it.

Supportive Employment. Mental health organizations and agencies often have supportive employment programs specifically for people who need a little extra help finding and keeping a job. In these programs, a counselor helps you create a resume, gives you interview tips, and assists with your job search. In some cases, you might "share" a job with someone else. This is a huge perk if you don't know if you'll feel up to going to work every day.

Limited-Income Jobs. If you receive government-funded Social Security or other disability benefits including Medicaid, you may need to keep your income below a certain amount. That doesn't mean that you can't work at all.

Make an appointment at your local Social Security office to find out exactly what your cap number is since it varies by state. Then you can enroll in a "Ticket to Work" program that offers services to help you find and keep a job (usually part-time) that won't jeopardize your benefits. You might also want to take advantage of the "gig economy" by working as a Lyft driver, becoming a TaskRabbit, or working small jobs for extra income.

REAL TALK:

66% of people surveyed have missed a day or more of work because of their mental health. Only 27% told their boss the truth about why they were out.

TAKING A MENTAL HEALTH DAY (OR THREE MONTHS)

If you start to feel overwhelmed by your work responsibilities, you should try to take a few days off to focus on your mental health. If you can, let your boss know a few days in advance when you'll be taking time off. You don't have to tell her why, specifically, you need to use your paid sick days or personal days.

Make the most of your mental health day by devoting some time to self-care. It's also a good idea to book yourself an extra therapy session for that day. Avoid the urge to stay in bed or binge watch Netflix all day. Zoning out by watching favorite shows might take your mind off work and life stress, but it won't send those calming signals to your brain the same way exercise or meditation does. And, yes, you may need to catch up on sleep, so allow yourself to sleep in, nap, and turn in early.

There may come a time when you need to take a chunk of time away from work for treatment. The Family Medical Leave Act (FMLA for short) was designed so that people can take up to twelve weeks off to deal with their medical issues or to take care of a family member, especially a newborn baby.

FMLA is an excellent option for people who are hospitalized or need to go to an addiction treatment center, but you don't have to be in a facility to take FMLA. You will probably need to provide documentation that you are getting treatment, but that doesn't mean you have to hand over your medical records.

Any company or organization that has more than fifty employees must grant you the leave. To be eligible for FMLA you must have worked at least twenty-four hours a week at your company over the past twelve months. Your boss may need to replace you, which is his problem, not yours. But when you return he must give you the same or almost identical job as the one you left.

FMLA leave is almost always unpaid, but your employer must continue your benefits while you are out. If you are getting deductions out of your paycheck for your health insurance, you'll probably have to write your company a check to keep them going after your paycheck has stopped.

It's nice if you can give the HR department a thirty-day head's up that you are going on FMLA, but it isn't required and may not be possible. When you are ready to return to work, your company may expect you to see a doctor of its choice to verify that you are healthy enough to return.

TALKING ABOUT YOUR MENTAL HEALTH AT THE OFFICE

I was working at *Cosmopolitan* when I was finally diagnosed with depression and anxiety. Even though my co-workers probably knew something was up, I didn't exactly feel comfortable sending a mass e-mail to the staff announcing that I was now taking an antidepressant and hoped I would be able to smile sometime soon. *Cosmo* was the type of place where we discussed our dating and sex lives during meetings, so there was no such thing as TMI. Still, I kept my diagnosis a secret. I was afraid that my co-workers would think I was weak—which is so ironic, since it takes a lot of strength to realize you need support and go out and get it. Slowly, I mentioned my depression to a few women I was close to and was surprised that some of them had been dealing with a disorder, too.

Today, I feel it's important to be vocal about my mental illness at work. My depression and anxiety don't affect my career any more than my asthma does—which means, I may take a sick day here and there and have extra doctor appointments, but that's it. It's admittedly easier for me to speak up now that I work in the behavioral health field, but when I mention my depression, no one blinks an eye. There are so many of us dealing with mental disorders—one-in-five to be exact—that, whether we are vocal about it or not, we're living it side by side.

GET INVOLVED WITH A CAUSE YOU CARE ABOUT

Allow me to drop some knowledge from my grandmother: "The best way to feel better is to do something nice for someone else." This advice has worked for me too many times to count.

When my brother was homeless, my therapist suggested that I volunteer with a homeless organization so that I could get a better understanding of what it was like to live on the streets or in a shelter. I imagined that I would join the outreach team of the Bowery Residents Committee, a nonprofit in New York City that tries to convince homeless people in the subway to go to one of its shelters. In reality, I was still very fragile and wouldn't have been much help to the team. Instead, the organization had an opening for a poetry teacher, and I just happened to have minored in poetry. I began teaching a poetry class in one of the shelters once a week for a few years. The experience helped me learn that people who were homeless were just people without a home. I hope it also helped *them* discover that poetry could speak to them, even at their lowest points, and that putting their own words on paper might give them strength. At the very least, we all got to read a lot of Charles Bukowski.

My grandmother and my therapist were on to something. Researchers have found that volunteering triggers the reward circuit in your brain, naturally making you happy. It can also lead to long-term contentment.

How to Volunteer

There are thousands of worthy causes out there and almost as many ways to support them. You can donate your time and work directly with people (or animals or the environment).

Ask yourself these four questions and then head over to a website that lists volunteer opportunities (try www.Idealist.org, www.Volunteermatch.org, or www.Dosomething.org) to get started.

What do you feel passionate about? If you are interested in mental health, you could participate in an awareness walk or become trained to volunteer at a crisis hotline. If animals are more your thing, call a local shelter and volunteer to spend time with strays. You can work toward change by joining a cause-based organization that advocates for reproductive rights, gun control, or whatever social issue you care about most.

What can you offer? Be creative about what you can offer an organization. Maybe you have excellent social media or video editing skills. Perhaps you can teach a class as I did. You can also volunteer your time to stuff envelopes (yes, that is still a thing), serve food, or do what the volunteer coordinator needs.

What can you *not* offer? Volunteer jobs are not one-size-fits-all. If money is tight for you and everyone you know, you probably aren't the best person to start a fundraiser. Some social service organizations, especially those that offer health care, may require that volunteers have completed a degree program or specialized training. It may be the case that a specific role (such as working directly with people who are homeless but resist the idea of going to a shelter) is too much of an emotional burden. That's OK. Find something else.

What would help *you*, too? Volunteering does not have to be an entirely selfless endeavor. Think about what you want to get out of the experience. Maybe you want to make friends or learn more about an issue you care about. If you know what you want to get out of the time you are giving away, you are more likely to do a good job and feel fulfilled at the same time.

DECIDING TO SHARE YOUR STORY

I decided to be open about my diagnosis of depression and anxiety several years after it was under control. By then, I was already working in the mental health field and knew it was unlikely I would ever be passed over for a job because I had announced to the world that I took an SSRI and saw a therapist. I also had a great support system, so it didn't bother me to know that my mental illness might change people's opinion about me.

I believe that the more people talk about their mental health openly, the better off we will all be—but there is no formula to help you decide when and if you should "come out" about your situation. And, you do need to be aware that there are some risks to sharing your story. Although it's illegal for schools, employers, or landlords to discriminate against you for having a mental illness, it is damn hard to prove that they are doing so in court.

I recommend starting your revelation slowly, maybe by telling your friends, then posting on your social media accounts until you are sure you are comfortable shouting it from the rooftops. If you aren't comfortable sharing your mental health status on social, you aren't ready.

Don't get me wrong, having a mental illness is absolutely nothing to be ashamed of. And I want you to feel the reward of making someone feel less alone. I just want you to be prepared so that you don't sacrifice your mental health in the process.

PART SEVEN

WHEN THE SHIT HITS THE FAN

Somewhere in between the time when you first start to experience symptoms, and when you're settled into a treatment plan that works, you may find yourself in a dark place. You may have been forced to spent time in a mental hospital or even tried to end your own life. Whatever happens, as bad as it may seem, you should know is that you aren't the only person who has ever gone through this. And with help—from your family and friends, mental health pros, and maybe even the government—you can get to the other side of it.

The stories you are about to read are from people who have experienced your worst nightmare. I hope they will inspire you during those tough times when the shit hits the fan.

"I WAS SENT TO A MENTAL HOSPITAL."

Sophia: *At the time, I basically lived to ski. Being an athlete was the most prominent part of my identity. I had been training since I was twelve and had made it onto my college cross-country ski team. Then, my freshman year, I got really sick. I was diagnosed with mono and chronic fatigue. I had a fever for an entire year. Suddenly, I couldn't exercise at all. I didn't know who was if I wasn't an athlete.*

I started spending more and more time in my dorm room bed and skipping class, which everyone was cool with at first because I had been sick for so long. Then, sleeping all day became the norm, and I had a hard time ever getting out of bed.

A close friend had killed himself the year before. I couldn't stop thinking about what it must have been like for him to be so alone that he would want to end it. I started thinking a lot about death. Actually, I wasn't just thinking about death; I considered ending my life too. I didn't want to be around anymore.

I knew I was depressed, but more than anything I felt helpless. Something motivated me to go to my campus health center. They referred me to an off-campus psychiatrist who thought I should be hospitalized at an inpatient facility in my college town. I felt like such shit at that point that I didn't care. It was nice to have someone tell me what to do. I was so out of it.

I spent the first two days in fetal position on my hospital bed. The girl I shared a room with was about my age, but I didn't want to talk to her. They started me on seizure medication and an antidepressant.

"What was so wrong with me that I couldn't deal with on my own?"

By the third day, I started to feel embarrassed. What was so wrong with me that I couldn't deal with on my own? It felt indulgent to be in a facility. It was too much. I met with a group every day. There were plenty of people my age who were there for all kinds of reasons. I knew I didn't belong, but when I told that to the psychiatrist who checked in with me every day, he just said it was the right place for me.

Some of my friends from school came by to visit, and I could tell they were overwhelmed and freaked out to see me like that. It didn't take long for my friendships with most of them to turn sour. I would find out later that one was a keeper.

Eventually, the medication started to kick in, and I did feel better. There was an activity room at the facility, so I began to make art, which was my major. I realized that I had to let go of the identity I had before and allow myself to create a new one.

After about a week, I was sent back to campus. I ended up withdrawing from all but one class that semester, and I quit the ski team. I was burned out mentally and physically. It was a relief not to have to worry about how poorly I was skiing. I thought about taking the spring semester off, but I didn't want to move back home. Plus, after only finishing one class during the fall, I didn't want to be further behind.

I was embarrassed about my hospitalization for a long time but, looking back, I'm glad I was there. Depression runs in my family, and even though I know there's no one-size-fits-all treatment, spending time in the hospital made me take it seriously. I feel lucky that my college helped me find the right resources for me when they did.

Sofia went on to get a BA and MFA in painting and is now a gallery supervisor at a university. She lives in New England with her husband, whom she met during her freshman year of college and their four-year-old daughter. She hits the slopes every chance she gets.

★ REAL TALK:

25% of people surveyed have spent the night in a mental hospital or rehab.

"I WAS ABUSED."

Erin: *I grew up to the sound of my mother screaming. She and my stepfather fought constantly, and their fights often turned violent. He would press her up against a wall and try to choke her. Sometimes she would run into my room and dial 911 into the phone while he banged on the door, but she would never actually make the call. When they weren't fighting, he was drinking. He would often down a keg of beer over four or five days. My mom was seething with anger and I was an easy target. I never knew when or why she would lash out at me next, but I always knew it was coming.*

Even though I had known him since I was two years old, I started to feel really uncomfortable around my stepfather when I became a teen. I later found out why. He had been taking pictures of me when he could get a good shot of my cleavage. One day I found a video camera that he had installed in my closet so he could watch me undress. I confronted him and my mom. He had some lame excuse, and my mom bought it. She told me, "If you think we should leave, you should know that you be will tearing this family apart." We did eventually leave, but it took several months and the suicide of my mom's brother for her to understand that life was too short to live this way.

Walking on eggshells was the only life I knew. My mom had a new boyfriend a month later, and since he lived in another town, I began spending my nights alone. Anxiety and loneliness were the only constants in my life. I tried to fill the void with sex. Turning myself into a sexual object was an easy way to get attention, but I still felt empty.

It took going away to college for me to get the distance I needed to process the trauma of my childhood and to face down the anxiety and depression I had been dealing with for so long. But it wasn't a smooth ride.

My freshman year was so lonely. I would go days without speaking to another human being. I hated putting myself out there. When I did speak up in class or start a conversation with someone I was constantly wondering what people were thinking about me. If I said something that made someone laugh, I would spend days wondering if it was funny or if they were just laughing at me.

I had been in therapy before, but I never felt comfortable enough with the therapist to open up. Luckily I found a psychologist in my college town who actually heard me, instead of just listening. She asked questions that really made me think about why I felt anxious and taught me how the trauma I had experienced in childhood impacted my relationships.

Through therapy, I've learned that I do deserve to be loved despite my flaws. Even though I've been with my boyfriend for three years, I still have a hard time vocalizing my emotions and being vulnerable. When I tell him not to touch me, he takes it personally. I also have an issue with being cuddled or touched *by other humans and get very anxious whenever I feel as though my boundaries aren't being respected. My cat Cali understands my boundaries and makes sure I never feel alone.*

I have learned to forgive my mom and stepfather–but I haven't forgotten the things they did. I believe that not forgetting will help me break the cycle in my own relationships.

"I believe that not forgetting will help me break the cycle in my own relationships."

Erin recently graduated from college and volunteers for mental health and suicide prevention organizations.

"I TRIED TO KILL MYSELF."

Alec: *I already wanted to die. I had just swallowed a bunch of pills. I was only fifteen, but it was my third suicide attempt. Then the cops showed up at my parent's house, along with a fire truck and an ambulance. It was like there was some catastrophe. I tried to run, but since cops surrounded our place, I didn't get very far. They tackled me to the ground and cuffed me. I rode to the hospital handcuffed to a gurney in the back of the ambulance.*

"It was like I had just committed some big crime."

They didn't have room for me in the hospital, so the police put me in a cop car and drove me to a hospital three hours away. It was like I had just committed some big crime.

Once we finally got to the hospital, they did a skin check and a strip search, looking for drugs or weapons. It was very degrading and over the top. The hospital staff was following protocol, but it made me feel like an object.

The first night was the hardest. I felt worse than I had when I tried to kill myself. At the same time, part of me was relieved to be around other people who would know what I was going through.

I spent most of my time there hanging out with the other kids in the adolescent unit, watching movies and playing games. After a couple of days, I started to get close to the other people there. That was honestly the best part. It's fine to talk to someone knows what you are going through because they read about it in a textbook, but it feels different when you are with people who are also trying to get better, even if they don't know how.

At the hospital, I had found people who understood what I was dealing with and others who were taking care of me. Leaving was so hard because I had to go back out into the world where everything was the same.

My psychiatrist started me on Prozac while I was in the hospital. No one told me that my depression would get a lot worse right after I started meds, and it didn't help that I missed a few days. I don't even remember the first few weeks because all I did was stay in my bed and cry. I wouldn't eat anything. My grandmother thought I was going to throw myself off the roof. But before long, I realized that I wasn't sad anymore.

I came out as gay when I was eight or nine, but I think it was pretty clear to everyone before that. For a while, I thought my sexual identity was connected to my mental disorders. It's true that people in the LGBTQ community have a higher rate of suicide attempts, and I've had suicidal thoughts for half my life. Now, I understand that struggling with your sexuality can create anxiety—and repressing the truth about it can make you feel depressed—but that's as far as the connection goes.

I don't have a mental disorder because I am gay. I am gay, and I have a mental disorder.

Alec is now studying special education and writing fiction. His novel *The Long Road Home* is a fictionalized account of his hospitalization. He is working on a sequel.

"I PUSHED EVERYONE AWAY."

Madison: *When I first started experiencing symptoms of depression, I alienated myself from everyone—even my family. I hardly ever left my house, much less made plans or stayed in touch with anyone. I hated myself and hated the way I felt. The shame and insecurity were too much, and I couldn't talk about my life or myself without feeling like some kind of fraud.*

My symptoms impact my relationships a lot. I am moody, flighty, irrationally sensitive, withdrawn, distracted, and sometimes straight-up cold and aloof. A lot of the time, I'm completely aware of how I'm behaving, but I can't seem to stop myself. It's like this self-destructive thing I do, and I end up pushing people I love away or saying things I don't mean and wouldn't say in my right mind.

Friends eventually lost touch, and my family stopped asking questions about my life. Because of this, I was very alone. I had only one friend who stood by my side during that time. We have been friends since I was fifteen. Instead of letting me freeze her out, she frequently checked in on me and kept me updated on her life. She would text to tell me she was on her way to my house, or just show up unannounced to hang out or drag me out to lunch or something. I used to hate it when she did stuff like that, but in retrospect, it saved our friendship.

"My go-to feeling is that everyone is against me and I don't need anyone."

I'm closer to my family now than I used to be, but I still distance myself from them when I go through a rough patch. My go-to feeling is that everyone is against me and I don't need anyone. It turns out that I'm actually happier when things are going well between us. It never works to combat feeling alone with isolating myself even more alone.

The people who I am closest to are a little more lenient and forgiving when I'm not my best self because they have a deeper understanding of my mental and emotional issues. I feel most supported when I feel understood—when people can honestly tell me that they don't think I'm broken or a monster. It's nice to be reminded that I'm human, and the reality is that I'm struggling with something that really warps my perception of the world and the role I play in it. When someone takes the time to listen to and understand my story and the stories of so many other people who go through this, it leads to the empathy and open-mindedness that every depressed or anxious person needs.

Madison has reconnected with her family and is in a relationship with someone who understands her and shows extreme patience when she is struggling with depression.

"I WENT TO REHAB."

Maya: I began using at age thirteen. I started with benzodiazepines like Klonopin and Ativan but later gravitated toward prescription painkillers like Vicodin and Percocet. At fourteen, addiction took over my life. Things started getting out of control my second semester of freshman year of high school when I *was using pills as a means of escape from the chaos of my life.*

I made it through my freshman year with decent grades, but they slipped pretty dramatically as my addiction worsened. I was struggling with anxiety, depression, and unresolved trauma. Without anyone or anything I felt I could turn to, the drugs gave me a sense of comfort and stability.

"I spent seventy-five days in the Utah desert learning about why I used."

Although my family had become very concerned about my drug use, it was ultimately me who asked to go to treatment. I went to a wilderness rehab program. I spent seventy-five days in the Utah desert learning about why I used, who I was, and what I wanted from recovery.

I have been blessed to have amazing psychiatrists who have helped me understand that it is common to deal with mental disorders and addiction. My drug use was heavily influenced by my extreme mood swings, which I learned were not a result of my failing at life as much as a chemical imbalance in my brain. I've taken many medications over the years—SSRIs, mood stabilizers, antipsychotics—but my doctors have told me it's relatively normal to have to semi-regularly switch medication since my body chemistry has changed so much since my early teens. Taking these medications has made a huge difference in my mood instability, depression, and anxiety.

After the wilderness program, I transitioned to an addiction treatment program in Salt Lake City where I stayed for sixteen months. I finished my sophomore and junior years of high school there. While it was hard to be away for so long and miss so much of the typical high school experience, I am so grateful that at such a young age I decided to invest in life-long recovery.

It certainly hasn't been a perfect road since I left rehab, but without the skills and experience I acquired there, I can't imagine where I'd be today.

Maya is now working on getting a BA in social work. She stays vigilant by going to twelve-step meetings, therapy, and hanging out with other people in recovery.

PART EIGHT

WHEN IT'S NOT YOU, IT'S...

In the introduction, I shared my story about trying to get help for my brother. Ultimately, I wasn't able to help him get treatment before he ended his life. I believe that if I'd known then what I know now, his life would not have ended so early. I think he would be thriving, like so many of the people with a mental disorder that you've read about in this book.

It has been bittersweet for me to learn about all of the ways we can help our loved ones since I lost mine. At times, I have blamed myself for not knowing more back then, or being able to do more. I simply did everything I possibly could at the time. That's all you can do, too.

This part of the book is packed with advice about how you can help someone recognize that they need support—including *actual words* to say when you need to have a tough conversation with a loved one. The goal is to prepare you to help someone you're concerned about, while also taking care of yourself. Keep in mind that there is no foolproof plan for this. Mental illness can be all kinds of shitty. It might temporarily change how people act and feel, but it doesn't change who they are. Try not to lose sight of the person you love.

HOW TO SUPPORT SOMEONE WITH A MENTAL ILLNESS

You have many reasons to be hopeful about the future of your loved one. There has never been a better time for someone with mental illness to get the treatment she needs to live a healthy and happy life. More people than ever have access to mental health care, and treatment is available for even the most severe illnesses. The stigma that was once a drumbeat is now more like a tapping foot.

When it comes to serious mental illness, including bipolar disorder and schizophrenia, the sooner she can get an official diagnosis and begin treatment (usually a combination of medication and therapy), the better the whole rest of her life will be.

Almost no one gets better on her own. When someone is struggling with a mental illness, she needs your compassion and support. But support is not the same as control. In most cases, unless your loved one is under eighteen, you can't make treatment decisions for her. You can learn about what she is dealing with, help her understand her options, and encourage her to give therapy and medication a try. You can drive her to therapy appointments and remind her to take medication. You can't take away her pain or force her to get treatment. You can't make her want to live. You can only love and support her, and respect the choices she makes.

LEARN ABOUT THE SYMPTOMS

It can be tricky to tell the difference between going through a rough patch and dealing with a mental disorder. You shouldn't plan on figuring out the diagnosis, but it's helpful to be able to understand the symptoms so that you can be specific about what concerns you. Start by familiarizing yourself with the symptoms of the mental disorders described in part one.

Some symptoms, such as sleeping too much, wanting more alone time, and acting recklessly, may be a standard operating procedure for teens and young adults. The key is to watch for patterns. You may want to check in with others to see if they have noticed similar symptoms.

HAVE "THE TALK"

Say: "I'm worried about your mental health. How are you feeling?"

When you feel ready to bring up your concerns, pick a time and place where you can have a private conversation. She may be embarrassed and even shed some tears. Feel free to enlist a few of her close friends or a family member if you think it will be helpful, but avoid a big intervention-style meet-up.

Start by letting her know that you care about her and want to be supportive. Try not to ask, "Is everything OK?" because that will make it harder for her to open up about what is wrong.

Instead, say, "I'm worried about your mental health. How are you feeling?"

It can be hard to point out what may seem to her like faults, but it's important to be honest about what you have noticed and why you are concerned. It won't help her to play down her problems. Bring up a few specific things, such as, "It seems like you haven't been sleeping much these past couple of weeks, and I know you've lost weight."

Try not to be discouraged if she doesn't immediately tell you what's been going on. For one thing, it can be hard for anyone to articulate new feelings that she might not even understand. Give her some time and then try again.

ENCOURAGE HER TO SEE A PRO

Say: "I've been thinking that a therapist might give you good advice on how to deal with your anxiety/mom/etc."

If she acknowledges that she is struggling, you should encourage her to see a psychiatrist or therapist. You want to avoid giving the impression that you are outsourcing your "good listener" duties. Instead, bring it up during a conversation about something else. You can say flat out, "I've been thinking that a therapist might give you good advice about how to deal with your anxiety/mom/etc." Keep your tone in check. Getting therapy is a positive step forward, so don't make it sound like calling an exterminator to get rid of bed bugs.

Even though therapy can be a totally transformative experience, there is still a little stigma attached to seeing a mental health pro. Therapists help people work through their feelings and make positive changes in their lives. Since good friends and family often do that very same thing—but over mimosas and without a co-pay—suggesting that she talk to someone else about her problems might make her feel as if you are tired of listening. Reassure her that a therapist can provide what even the closest friend cannot. Unlike you, therapists are trained to understand her underlying issues, and they have the know-how to help her address and change her negative thought and behavior patterns and work through her pain.

Make the Connection to Care Smoother

Say: "I'd be happy to help you look for a therapist."

Make the whole process of reaching out for help less intimidating by sharing your own experiences or suggesting a few not-too-threatening things she might want to talk about for starters. It might help to remind her that one session will take less than an hour of her time. She doesn't have to commit to anything more than that unless she wants to.

You can help further by offering to make a list of mental health pros in your area or driving her to the appointment. You might even want to propose a post-therapy date at your favorite restaurant.

Be Patient

Ultimately, someone with a mental illness has to decide for herself to take medication and do the therapeutic work to manage the symptoms. That can be hard for anyone to do, especially someone who is still learning how to be herself in the world.

There's a chance that she may need to cut back on hours at work or even take a break from school or college. Almost every person I interviewed for this book talked about how embarrassing and disappointing it was to do this, especially as they watched their friends move forward. Try not to fixate on what she should be doing at this point in her life. Allow her some time and space to focus on what she can do to manage her symptoms and take care of her mental and physical health.

Reset Your Expectations

When someone you love is hurting, it's natural to want to do everything you can to make the pain stop ASAP. Unfortunately, there is no quick or easy fix for mental illness. This will also require patience with *yourself*, because your relationship with her may never be quite the same again. It will suck at times, but your unconditional love can help pull her through.

As hard as it will be at times, try to avoid getting upset or angry about things she does because of her symptoms. That doesn't mean that you should allow her to act like a jerk; you can and *should* set expectations—but make sure they are realistic, given her mental disorder.

Prepare for a Crisis

If she is has a psychotic episode, or you think she might hurt herself or someone else, you'll have to act quickly. Although people with mental disorders very rarely become violent, when someone doesn't have control of her thoughts, you do need to be prepared for a mental health crisis. Start by making a list of contact information for her psychiatrist, doctor, and therapist, along with any medication she is taking.

Add 911 to your list, and in a case where you feel she may be endangering herself or someone else, dial it pronto and request a mental health or wellness check. In most states, if the crisis intervention team (often made up of police officers) agrees that this person is likely to become violent in the next hours or days, they will hospitalize her for seventy-two hours.

Consider an Advance Directive

People who have bipolar disorder, schizophrenia, schizoaffective disorder, or major depression may benefit from having a *psychiatric advance directive*. Like a health care directive or living will, this is an outline of a person's treatment preferences. It identifies who she wants to monitor the situation and help ensure that she receives the preferred treatment during a mental health crisis. (Even the definition of *crisis* can be specified here.)

Learn to Deal with Relapses

Say: "I believe that you can make it through this. I'm still here for you."

Getting on a treatment plan that works rarely happens without a few false starts. It's not unusual for someone to have an on/off again relationship with therapy and medication for a while. As frustrating as it may be, you may have to restart your action plan again and again.

Real Talk:

Worried? We've all been there. 97% of people surveyed said they have been concerned about someone's mental health. Of those, 87% were worried for a friend, 54% a parent, 50% a sibling, 45% a significant other, and 20% a coworker.

WHEN IT'S NOT YOU, IT'S...

Labels can be limiting. Some people are actual siblings but have more of a parent-child thing going on. Some friends are more like family, and co-workers more like friends. You know the truth of your relationship. Let it be your guide as you read this section.

Your Kid

If your child is under eighteen, you are in a golden window of time when you can still make the rules and decisions regarding his mental health care—at least according to the government. If he is over eighteen but still on your insurance, you may be able to maintain some level of control. Do everything you can to get him into care while you are still paying the bills. The longer he lives with an untreated mental disorder, the less likely it is that he will be able to pay his own therapy bills.

Take Family Trip to the Doc. It's best to find a therapist or psychiatrist who your kid connects with, but if he has a good relationship with your family doctor, you might want to start there. Be sure that you also spend some time with the pro, either in an initial call or e-mail, to share what you have experienced. This shouldn't be a family therapy session, but it won't help anyone if your kid insists that everything is fine.

Keep a Symptom Journal. It can be hard to get a diagnosis when the patient is young, because the *DSM* diagnostic criteria are based on a pattern of behavior, sometimes requiring that symptoms be present for six months. You might want to keep a journal of your kid's behavior so you can note how it changes over time. Some mental health pros are against "labeling" patients, but an overwhelming majority of people I've interviewed feel that receiving a diagnosis is really empowering. It can also point to the right medication.

Sign Up for Family Education. Far and away the most helpful thing a parent of someone with a mental disorder can do is to get in touch with the local chapter of the National Alliance on Mental Illness (NAMI). There are chapters in almost every state and city across the country, and most offer a free program called Family-to-Family. Part support group and part psychology master class, it's designed to help families learn how to best support their kids while keeping the peace at home. As a bonus, NAMI chapters usually have a few whizzes who know everything there is to know about their state's mental health laws. (Find your state's NAMI chapter in part ten.)

YOUR SIGNIFICANT OTHER

Married people and domestic partners will probably have more influence with their SO than those who have been dating for a few months. But, no matter how serious your relationship is, if your significant other is struggling with a mental disorder, he is probably feeling less lovable.

Show Your Love. If there is anything scarier than not being in control of your mind, it's that the person you love will stop loving you. The biggest thing you can do when your partner is struggling is to show him again and again that you love and support him.

Keep Up the Support. It's hard to watch someone you care about deal with a mental disorder. On bad days, he might be overcome by his symptoms and less than fun to be around; and on good days, he might be so into taking care of his own mental health that you end up as his last priority. It's almost impossible not to feel hurt, but be patient and remember to take care of yourself first. You may want to see your own therapist for extra support.

Make Self-Care a Date. One way to show your SO that you are there for him is to help him get healthier. Instead of bar hopping on the weekend, plan to go to a yoga class together or see a movie. Prepare healthy meals instead of ordering in pizza. These small things can add up in a big way.

Protect Yourself. Mental disorders aren't an excuse for domestic violence. If your partner ever hits or abuses you, get help immediately.

YOUR FRIEND

Ironically, one of the first things people do when they are struggling with their mental health—and need support the most—is push people away. Maybe they are embarrassed or don't want to burden their pals with all of their sadness and anxiety. In a case like that, be a real friend and hang in there. Don't assume someone else is "on it."

Just Listen. It's easy to get caught up in your own life and miss the signs that your friend is trying to reach out to you. Sometimes people are better at sharing what is actually going on with them than we are at listening—so if you have a friend in need, stay vigilant. When he does share, avoid simplifying his problems or minimizing his pain. Start by really listening.

Stay in Touch. There's a good chance your friend may not feel like hanging out for a while—and he may be a little bit of a drag when he does. Even when you are totally annoyed by his behavior, stay close. A quick text saying, *"Hey, just checking in to let you know I'm here for you"* can go a long way toward lifting your friend up, even if he doesn't text you back.

YOUR SIBLING

Some brothers and sisters have an incredible bond and ESP-like levels of communication; others barely talk to each other if they can avoid it. If you're reading this book to learn more about how your sibling can manage his or her life with a mental disorder, and how you can help, you are probably closer to the former.

Call a Family Meeting. If you have supportive and capable parents, go to them first. They may already have a plan in place to help your brother deal with his mental disorder, or at least be

PART 8: WHEN IT'S NOT YOU, IT'S...

open to working on one together. But if like many of us, your family is more of a patchwork of people with varying degrees of empathy and ability to take care of others, you may find yourself stepping into a more parental role. No matter the situation, talk to your family about what you have noticed and see if they have similar concerns. This can help you identify patterns of symptoms, such as if your bro has been sad or pissed off every day for no obvious reason.

Your Parent

It's unusual for someone to be diagnosed with mental illness after age forty-five, but it does happen. Most likely, your parent has been dealing (or not dealing) with his symptoms for a long time. It's not your fault that your parent is struggling. You can't take away the pain, but you can make life a little easier.

Take Extra Good Care of Yourself. The most important thing you can do for your parent is to make sure you are taking care of *yourself*. If dad is dealing with a mental disorder and unable to take good care of you and your siblings, you may end up with a lot of extra responsibility you didn't ask for. You're going to have to be in fighting shape for that. That means eating well, getting enough sleep, and finding time for self-care.

Ask for Help. When your home is chaotic, it's hard to deal with school, work, and everything else in your life. Remember that you aren't in this alone. Now is the time to lean on your other

EVERYTHING IS GOING TO BE OK

parent (even if your mom and dad aren't together), grandparents, family friends, friends' parents, neighbors, teachers—really, any adult you trust. You don't have to share every detail of your family's problems; it's enough to let them know that your parent is having a hard time and you could use a little help.

Your Co-worker

Talking about mental health may be taboo where you work, but it can be exactly what someone needs to get help. At their lowest moments, many people—myself included—think that as long as they are showing up to work (or getting good grades in school), they don't need to get help. In a case like that, the person most likely to make a difference is someone at work. As a co-worker or supervisor, you can play an important role in helping a colleague, but the lines can quickly become blurred regarding what is helpful, hurtful, or even illegal.

Watch Your Attitude. When in doubt, think about how you would handle the situation if you knew (or suspected) your co-worker had cancer. Would you want to make him feel supported? Absolutely. Would you complain to your boss when he called in sick, again? Probably not. Of course, this litmus test does have its limits; for one thing, people aren't usually ashamed of getting cancer. But you get the point: People who are struggling need and deserve our support. Be respectful, and sensitive to your language. Avoid saying things like, "I'm going crazy" or, "The boss is acting psycho today." Retire all jokes about

214

wanting to kill yourself, including the not-so-hilarious pointer finger to the temple.

Respect Your Colleague's Rights. Mental illness can lead to discrimination at work. No matter what the diagnosis is, it is illegal to fire someone, reject him for a job or promotion, or force him to take medical leave. As a supervisor, you are only allowed to ask about someone's health (including their mental health) if the employee has asked for accommodations under the Americans with Disabilities Act. (Read more about that in part six), or if you think his medical condition may make it impossible or unsafe for her to do her job.

Create a Safe Space for a Private Convo. It's really best to encourage your employee or co-worker to tell you about her issues. You can make it easier for her to open up by having coffee, lunch, or even a drink outside of your workplace. Once you are settled somewhere together, ask a general question like, "How is life treating you these days?" If she begins to open up, let her know that your conversation will be confidential. And mean it. Depending on your relationship, you may feel comfortable asking if she has considered talking to a therapist. You might want to share a story of someone you know (or someone you read about in this book) who has been through a similar experience.

Know When to Raise a Flag. There are two exceptions to the privacy rule: If your employee or co-worker is talking about wanting to end his life or putting others directly at risk, you should absolutely speak up about it to your boss or someone in the HR department, ASAP.

✳ REAL TALK:

What We Wish Everyone Knew About Mental Health

Here's what young adults with mental illness want the world to be woke to.

- *"It's not just about trying to get attention."*
- *"Some things happen to our minds and bodies that we just can't control."*
- *"You can't just switch it on and off."*
- *"It can happen to anybody."*
- *"I didn't choose this, and I'm not using it as an excuse."*
- *"Mental health is just as important as physical health."*
- *"It's OK to talk about it."*
- *"People often think that mental health requires only a good attitude and positive thinking. These things help, but they do not make mental illness go away."*
- *"It is often more complex than a single diagnosis, and there is so much overlap between symptoms that it is difficult to*

pin down a single illness."

- *"Mental illness isn't just about feeling bad—it's more like a low-grade state of existence that touches every part of your life."*

- *"It's an illness, not a character flaw."*

- *"Having a mental illness does not mean that you are less of a person."*

- *"It is as real and valid as cancer, diabetes, AIDS, and any other physiological conditions you can think of."*

- *"Mental illness is incredibly common. It's more than just anxiety or depression. The 'scary' disorders are common too."*

- *"It's not anyone's fault."*

SUPPORT YOURSELF TOO

You have to put on your oxygen mask before you can help someone else with his. It's a cliché because it's true. Even if your heart is breaking to the point where you'd like to trade places with your loved one so you could take his pain away, you still have to take care of yourself first. In this context, the "oxygen mask" really means taking care of your own mental and physical health.

If you are living with someone who is dealing with a serious mental illness, you are in for a marathon of challenges and setbacks. Your mission is to take the very best care of yourself that you can. If you effectively take care of yourself, you'll be better able to help your loved out when times are tough and be in a good space to enjoy the happy moments when they arise. And they will.

How will you know if you are taking good enough care of yourself? Your body will let you know. If you keep getting headaches, feel exhausted, have an upset stomach, trouble sleeping, or unexplained aches and pains, it's a sign that your mental health may be out of whack and you need to step up your self-care game.

Your Self-Care Checklist

To make sure you are taking the best possible care of yourself, run down this list regularly and check the boxes.

Exercise daily. You don't have to clock in at the gym; a brisk walk will do.

Eat healthy meals. A well-balanced combo of fruits, veggies, lean protein, and whole grains will keep your energy up and boost your mood.

Get seven-to-nine hours of sleep each day. I say "day" because naps count, but obviously, most of your high-quality shut-eye should come at night. Try to keep your bedtime as regular as possible.

Stay sober. Avoid binge drinking and drugs. As tempting as it might be to get blasted so you can forget your situation for just a few hours, it will actually make the stress you feel even worse as soon as the buzz wears off. Not worth it.

Relax. Whether it is meditation, deep breathing, yoga, or getting a massage, use any relaxation technique that seems to provide the headspace you need to think clearly.

Stay connected. With the outside world, that is. This is especially important if you spend a lot of time with someone who isn't in touch with reality. Even if no one knows or understands what you are going through, spending a little time connecting with others will help you stay grounded.

Find Support. NAMI has support group chapters in almost every state and city across the country. (Find yours in part ten.) If groups aren't your thing keep it one-on-one and talk to a therapist.

Get grateful. You might not be feeling very #blessed at the moment, but taking time each day to find one thing to be thankful for (even if it's, "We all stayed alive today") will help you keep things in perspective.

Avoid guilt. If you're caught up in the "why him and not me?" mind trap or daydream about what it would be like if your loved one were "normal," you might have a case of survivor's guilt. We've all been there. Try to avoid judging yourself. You have enough going on.

PART NINE

SAVE YOUR OWN LIFE

SURVIVE THE NEXT TWO MINUTES

Right now, you may be feeling so incredibly sad that living doesn't seem worth it. You are tired of feeling worthless, helpless, and alone. You just want this pain to end. You may be thinking that the only way out—the only way to stop feeling so much pain—is to end your life.

Maybe you think no one would really and truly care if you were gone. Or maybe it would serve them right for not understanding how much you were hurting. At least you wouldn't hurt anymore. You may even be thinking about how you would do it.

If this sounds true for you, I want you to know that I have been there. I may have had different reasons for wanting to end my life, but the pain you are in right now—that feeling—I know it. It is universal. *You are not alone.*

You are not as alone as you feel. You are loved. Take a deep breath in, exhale, and try to let that sink in. *You are loved.*

I don't know when your pain will end. I don't have those answers, and you don't have to have the answers right now, either. You just have to believe that the pain *will* end. *This pain is temporary.* Repeat it until you believe it.

Your life matters. It matters to me. And I know, deep down, that it matters to you. It matters to all of the people who are literally waiting by the phone right this minute for you to call. They want to talk to you so that, together, you can make a plan to stay safe. Pick a crisis hotline and make the call. Right now, you have the power to save your own life just by reaching out to someone who is already waiting to hear from you.

You are not alone. You are loved. Your life matters.

REASONS TO STAY
a very helpful list

1. You won't end the pain. You will just pass it along to the people who love you and will be broken by your death.

2. Music.

3. There will be another Star Wars movie worth waiting for.

4. Your future children.

5. Almost everyone who has attempted suicide (eventually) became so glad they are still here.

6. To crush it at your high school reunion.

7. Someone in this world needs you.

8. Kittens.

9. You can use your life to help people who are struggling.

10. All the good books you haven't read yet.

11. Your dream is out there. Think about how amazing it will feel when you find it!

12. Guitars.

13. The people who love you. Yes, they exist.

14. Puppies.

15. Knowing this too shall pass.

16. Yoga.

17. You only have to make it through today.

18. Sex with someone you actually love.

19. To see the world become a better place, because slowly but surely, it is.

20. _____.   ← FILL IN THE BLANK!

hi my name is:

#KILLINGIT

GOOD.
SO GOOD...
worth it!

EVERYTHING IS GOING TO BE OK

NUMBERS TO SAVE IN YOUR PHONE

These free hotlines are basically the Ghostbusters of mental health. They will pick up whenever you need to talk, chat, or text.

- **Crisis Text Line: Text "Start" to 741-741**

  The Crisis Text Line is the first crisis hotline to operate completely via text. Its volunteers are trained to help you get out of panic mode and into a calm place. Just text from your cell anytime and a counselor will jump right in.

- **National Suicide Prevention Lifeline: 1-800-273-8255 or chat at www.Suicidepreventionlifeline.org**

  You don't have to be suicidal to contact the Lifeline. The counselors are trained to talk you through a crisis and can connect you to local resources in your area. If the phone isn't your style, you can chat with a counselor on the Lifeline's website.

- **National Sexual Assault Network: 1-800-656-4673 or chat at www.Rainn.org**

  If you are a victim of sexual assault or abuse, the counselors at RAINN have your back. Call their confidential support line for emotional support and help to figure out next steps.

- **The Trevor Project: 1-866-488-7386 or text "Trevor" to 1-202-304-1200 or chat at www.Trevorproject.org**

  The Trevor Project provides crisis services to LGBTQ people between the ages of thirteen and twenty-four. But don't worry if you happen to be a little older—they aren't going to card you.

- **Veterans Crisis Line: 1-800-273-8255, text 838255, or chat at www.Veteranscrisisline.net**

  This hotline was created by Veterans Affairs specifically

to provide free, confidential support to veterans and their family. Some of the crisis counselors are veterans themselves, and all of them understand the complex issues people deal with after serving.

MAKE A PLAN TO STAY SAFE

One the best things you can do for yourself is to create a plan to get you through the tough moments. In the suicide prevention world, it's called a safety plan. The gist is that when you find yourself struggling, you whip out the plan and go down the list of things to do, people to reach out to, and places to go until you have gotten out of your dark place.

It's a good idea to create the plan with your therapist so he or she can make sure it's realistic and effective—but if that isn't an option, go ahead and DIY. Use the space below, or grab your journal, laptop, maybe even the Notes app on your phone. If apps are more your style, you can download a free safety planning app called My3 from the App Store or Google Play.

ID YOUR TRIGGERS

Write down all of the things that make you want to die. Maybe it's a thought, such as, "I'm a loser," or a situation that you hate, like fighting with a person you love. It could be feeling super depressed or regretting something you've done.

My triggers are...

1.

2.

3.

USE YOUR COPING SKILLS

Make a list of at least three things you can do by yourself to take your mind off of everything you just listed. Since you probably have your phone with you, check out the app Virtual Hope Box which can help you relax and take your mind off things. Your coping strategies don't have to be healthy; they just have to distract you for a little bit. (In case you are drawing a blank, some of my go-to coping strategies are journaling, going for a run, and carbo-loading.)

When I feel triggered, I can...

1.

2.

3.

KNOW YOUR SAFE SPACES

Think about places you can go where you feel safe—somewhere you can "reset" your mind. Maybe it's a park, place of worship, or—my personal favorite—the children's section of a bookstore. Write down three.

My safe places are...

1.

2.

3.

Find your people

Make a list of at least three people who you can talk to about anything, day or night. Write down their numbers. If you can't think of three, use the crisis hotlines.

The people I know I can talk to when I'm at a breaking point are...

1.

2.

3.

Call on the pros

Write down the names and numbers of your mental health pros, local hospital, and urgent-care facility.

If I think I might try to hurt myself, I will contact...

1.

2.

3.

4. National Suicide Prevention Lifeline, 1-800-273-8255

Get yourself out of harm's way

Make a list of anything you might use to take your own life so you can tell someone about them when you are struggling. That might mean asking someone to hold on to your pill stash or gun for a while.

I will ask others to help me stay safe by...

1.

2.

REMEMBER YOUR REASONS FOR LIVING

Maybe it's your family, your dream of becoming a famous photographer someday, or that you love listening to music. Whatever it is, write down what will keep you going when you feel like giving up.

The most important things to me are...

1.

2.

3.

HELP SOMEONE SAVE THEIR LIFE

It would be so much easier if humans were like cars, and came with a set of warning lights that could blink on to alert the world that we are "Out of gas," "Need TLC, STAT," or, "Really thinking about ending it." Until Apple comes up with that, we'll just have to rely on listening to other people and paying attention to their words and actions.

Even the act of listening can be tricky, though, because people don't always say what they mean or mean what they say. Think about how many times you've heard someone grumble, "I want to kill myself," because the copier jammed or she forgot her phone at home. Maybe she even made that gun-to-the-head gesture to emphasize her annoyance. For some reason, we are totally cool with jokes about suicide but often miss the signals when someone is actually thinking about ending her life.

You don't have to wait until someone you care about is suicidal to step up and help. Learning the risk factors can help you understand why someone might feel that her life isn't worth living. There are warning signs you can be on the lookout for and simple questions you can ask to get a life-saving conversation started.

SUICIDE IS PREVENTABLE

The Center for Disease Control (CDC) (the government agency that has the morbid job of keeping track of such things), announced that in 2016, the suicide rate had risen to a thirty-year high. While the numbers were higher in all demographics other than the seventy-five-or-older crowd, the number of people between age fifteen and forty-four who took their lives increased by forty-seven percent!

Every single one of those deaths was preventable. Mental health problems, the loss of a loved one from death or a break-up, and addiction are major risk factors for suicide. The more risk factors someone has, the more likely he is to take his own life. Getting treatment and support for those issues—and having a stellar support system in general—can help build up someone's resilience, which works like a superpower to weaken those risk factors.

Here's the full list of risk factors for suicide:

- Untreated mental illness
- Addiction
- Loss of a loved one from death or a break-up
- Hopelessness
- Impulsive or aggressive tendencies
- History of trauma or abuse
- Major physical illness
- Previous suicide attempt
- Family history of suicide
- Job loss
- Easy access to guns
- Isolation
- Stigma associated with asking for help

- Cultural or religious belief that suicide is a "noble resolution" of a personal or political dilemma
- Exposure to others who have died by suicide (IRL or via the media)

Know the Warning Signs

There is a difference between joking about suicide, thinking about suicide, and actually *being suicidal*. When someone is suicidal, he not only wants to die but is working on a plan to end his life. When someone you care about is suicidal, it's incredibly important to get help immediately. The National Suicide Prevention Lifeline has five CDC-approved steps to prevent suicide. Learn them at www.Bethe1to.com.

How can you tell if somebody you know might be suicidal? These are the warning signs to look for:

- Talking about wanting to die or kill himself
- Looking for a way to kill herself, such as buying a gun or Googling "how to die"
- Talking about feeling as if he has no reason to live
- Upping her use of alcohol or drugs
- Saying he feels trapped by unbearable pain
- Talking about being a burden to others
- Behaving recklessly
- Sleeping way too little or too much
- Going into isolation mode
- Exhibiting rage or a desire to seek revenge

"WHAT DO I SAY WHEN SOMEONE TELLS ME SHE WANTS TO DIE?"

It's scary when someone you love (or, hell, even a stranger) says that she wants to end her life. Try not to panic. It's a big deal that your friend confided in you—and you *can* help her. A lot of people feel suicidal sometimes; that doesn't mean they will act on it. But it's not your job to figure out whether she will or won't. The best thing you can do in a situation like that is to connect your friend to a pro who *can* figure it out.

The first thing you should do when someone expresses suicidal thoughts is to make sure she feels supported. Say something like, "I'm really glad you told me. I know this is hard to talk about." If you are willing to go a little deeper, try letting your friend know that you care by saying something along the lines of, "I'm concerned about you. I want to help you get through this." Then you can ask, "Is there anything I can do to help you feel better?"

You may need to let her talk about why she wants to die. Listen and respond, but remember that you aren't a therapist. Offer to do simple things that won't overwhelm your friend, such as keeping her company or calling someone who can.

Her immediate safety is the biggest issue. Try asking, "Are you thinking of hurting yourself right now?" If the answer is *yes*, you should call a crisis hotline or 911 right away. Of course, there's a good chance your friend is telling you about this via text or chat—which means you might not be able to tell if she is serious or just being sarcastic. You might want to call just to hear her voice—but whether you are talking or texting, try probing a little deeper and ask her to say more about her feelings.

The bottom line is this: If someone tells you she wants to kill herself, it is not your job (or within your ability) to save her. Helping her get qualified help and support ASAP is the absolute best thing you can do.

Take Care of Yourself, Too

Supporting someone who is thinking about suicide can be very stressful, and you should absolutely get help for yourself. You can start by adding a few self-care activities into your day so that you don't become depleted. If you do begin to feel overwhelmed, reach out to your own support network or your therapist.

My go-to for support is the National Suicide Prevention Lifeline. I worked there for years, so I know that there are hundreds of trained crisis counselors ready and willing to support you through your darkest moments. (In case you were wondering, they are the people behind Logic's smash hit, "1-800-273-8255.") You can call them about yourself or someone else, or even if you have some questions about something troubling that a friend has been saying. If you're freaked out about anything having to do with suicide, these people can help right away.

PART TEN

RESOURCES

One of the trickiest parts of navigating the mental health care system is that services and laws vary by state. The final part of the book includes national organizations along with a state-by-state list of government agencies and nonprofits that offer a range of services to help you. There's also a glossary that explains all those code words you'll come across and a reference guide so you can dig deeper.

HOTLINES

Need some real-time support? Some are crisis hotlines that you can call or text, some are information lines that can direct you to services, but all have real, live humans standing by, waiting to help you.

Crisis

Crisis Text Line: Text "Start" to 741-741

Disaster Distress Helpline: 1-800-985-5990 or text "Talk-WithUs" to 66746

Drug Abuse National Helpline: 1-800-662-4357

Love is Respect: 1-866-331-9474 or text "loveis" to 22522*

National Domestic Violence Hotline: 1-800-799-SAFE (7233)

National Suicide Prevention Lifeline: 1-800-273-TALK (8255)

RAINN's National Sexual Assault Hotline: 1-800-656-HOPE (4673)

The Trevor Project: 1-866-488-7386 or text "Trevor" to 1-202-304-1200

Veterans Crisis Line: 1-800-273-8255, press 1 or text 838255

Information

National Alliance on Mental Illness Information Hotline: 1-800-950-NAMI (6264)

National Eating Disorders Association Helpline: 1-800-931-2237

Substance Abuse and Mental Health Services National Helpline: 1-800-662-HELP (4357)

NATIONAL ORGANIZATIONS

This is a list of the MVPs that offer support, raise awareness, and advocate for people dealing with a mental disorder, eating disorder, or addiction. If you're interested in getting involved with a charity or want to have a career in mental health, they are all good places to start. By no means does this represent all government agencies and organizations that focus on mental health. I've only included groups that provide resources directly to you.

Active Minds

Active Minds is an organization supporting mental health awareness and education for students with chapters on more than 450 high school and college campuses.

www.activeminds.org

Alcoholics Anonymous (AA)

AA is a 12-step support group for people with substance use disorder. There are specialized groups for specific addictions like alcohol and narcotics, as well as groups for families.

www.aa.org

Bazelon Center for Mental Health Law

The Bazelon Center for Mental Health Law is an organization that aims to protect the rights of adults and children with mental illness and developmental disabilities through policy development and public education. They also offer legal assistance to people facing discrimination.

www.bazelon.org

Bring Change to Mind

Created by actress Glenn Close and her sister Jessie, Bring Change to Mind raises awareness about mental illness through public education and advocacy. They offer advice on how to talk about mental health and have programs for high schools and colleges.

www.bringchange2mind.org

Clubhouse International

Clubhouse International is the sister organization of Fountain House, a community that helps people with serious mental illness make friends, learn new skills, and achieve their employment and educational goals. You can find the closet clubhouse near you on their website.

www.clubhouse-intl.org

Crisis Text Line

Crisis Text Line is an organization with a sole purpose of helping young adults in crisis, via text message. Its volunteers are trained to help you get out of panic mode and into a calm place.

www.crisistextline.org

Depression and Bipolar Support Alliance (DBSA)

DBSA hosts more than 650 support groups, online and IRL, for people dealing with depression and bipolar disorder nationwide.

www.dbsalliance.org

Facing Addiction & National Council on Alcoholism and Drug Dependence (NCADD)

NCADD has partnered with Facing Addiction to prevent addiction and connect people to substance use disorder treatment.

www.ncadd.org

International OCD Foundation

This organization raises awareness about OCD and expands access to treatment through providing research grants and training programs. You can find a support group on their website.

www.iocdf.org

Jed Foundation

The Jed Foundation helps teens and young adults, plus their families and educators, navigate the transition to adulthood. Their website is chock full of information specifically about college mental health.

www.jedfoundation.org

Love is Respect

This organization helps young adults prevent and end abusive relationships by offering a 24/7 crisis and text line.

www.loveisrespect.org

Mental Health America

Mental Health America helps people recognize early symptoms of mental illness and get access to treatment. You can take a screening quiz on their website to find out if you should reach out for support.

www.mentalhealthamerica.net

Military One Source

Consider this a one-stop shop, open 24/7, that offers support and provides resources to people in the military and their families.

www.militaryonesource.mil

National Alliance on Mental Illness (NAMI)

NAMI has chapters in almost every state that offer support groups and workshops to people with mental illness and their families. The organization also works to improve public policy, raise awareness, and provide support via its online community and information hotline.

www.nami.org

National Association of Anorexia Nervosa and Associated Disorders (ANAD)

ANAD assists people struggling with eating disorders by providing education and support for families, schools, and people dealing with an eating disorder.

www.anad.org

National Eating Disorders Association (NEDA)

NEDA supports people affected by eating disorders by hosting support groups, raising awareness about prevention, and making connections to treatment.

www.nationaleatingdisorders.org

National Education Alliance for Borderline Personality Disorder (NEABPD)

NEABPD provides education, raises awareness, and promotes research to enhance the quality of life for people with borderline personality disorder. They also offer educational courses for families.

www.borderlinepersonalitydisorder.com

National Institute on Alcohol Abuse and Alcoholism

This federal agency has a treatment navigator to help people with substance use disorder get support.

www.niaaa.nih.gov

Project 375

Created by NFL player Brandon Marshall, Project 375 raises awareness about mental illness and provides in-person mental health first aid trainings.

www.project375.org

Substance Abuse and Mental Health Services (SAMHSA)

SAMHSA is the federal agency that funds the National Suicide Prevention Lifeline and basically all of the government's national addiction and mental health treatment programs. You'll find all of those resources on their website.

www.samhsa.gov

Schizophrenia and Related Disorders Alliance of America (SARDAA)

SARDAA provides peer-to-peer support groups, education, and information to people with schizophrenia and related disorders.

www.sardaa.org

Treatment Advocacy Center

This advocacy organization promotes policies to help people with serious mental illness get treatment. Its website is filled with guides and tools to help people understand the specific treatment laws in their state.

www.treatmentadvocacycenter.org

The Trevor Project

The Trevor Project provides crisis intervention and suicide prevention services to LGBTQ people between ages thirteen to twenty-four. They have a hotline, text line, chat, and online community.

www.thetrevorproject.org

National Suicide Prevention Lifeline

The Lifeline is a network more than 160 local crisis centers nationwide who are trained to talk you through a crisis and can connect you to local resources in your area. You can also chat with a counselor on the Lifeline's website.

www.suicidepreventionlifeline.org

Rape, Abuse & Incest National Network (RAINN)

RAINN is an anti-sexual violence organization that carries out programs to prevent sexual violence, help survivors, and ensures that perpetrators are brought to justice. They also operate the National Sexual Assault Hotline.

www.rainn.org

Veterans Crisis Line

The Veterans Crisis Line connects veterans in crisis (and their families) to helpers at the Department of Veterans Affairs via hotline, online chat, or text.

www.veteranscrisisline.net

RESOURCES IN YOUR STATE

Every state has a department of health that is responsible for improving the overall health of its residents. They do this through public awareness campaigns and programs to target specific issues like preventing obesity by educating the public about calorie counts or helping people stop smoking by offering free smoking cessation programs. Many states have realized that mental health and addiction are a big deal, and have created branches specifically for those services.

The following directory includes the name and website for the office in your state so you can find out what services are available. There's also a 211 in just about every state that can connect you to those resources. It's like 911, but not for emergencies. When possible, I've included the National Association of Mental Illness (NAMI) state chapters which may offer local support groups in your area.

Alabama

Alabama Department of Mental Health www.mh.alabama.gov

Alabama NAMI www.namialabama.org

Alabama 211 www.211connectsalabama.org

Alaska

Alaska Department of Health and Social Services - Division of Behavioral Health www.dhss.alaska.gov/dbh

Alaska NAMI www.namialaska.org

Alaska 211 www.alaska211.org

Arizona

Arizona Department of Health Services www.azdhs.gov

Arizona NAMI www.namiarizona.org

Arizona 211 www.211arizona.org

Arkansas

Arkansas Department of Human Services - Division of Behavioral Health Services www.humanservices.arkansas.gov/about-dhs/dbhs

Arkansas NAMI www.namiarkansas.org

Arkansas 211 www.arkansas211.org

California

California Department of Health Care Services - Mental Health Services www.dhcs.ca.gov

California Department of Health Care Services - Substance Use Disorder Services www.dhcs.ca.gov/provgovpart/Pages/SUD-Directories.aspx

California NAMI www.namica.org

Colorado

Colorado Department of Human Services www.colorado.gov/pacific/cdhs

Colorado Crisis Services www.coloradocrisisservices.org

Colorado NAMI www.namicolorado.org

Colorado 211 211colorado.communityos.org

Connecticut

Connecticut Department of Mental Health and Addiction Services www.ct.gov/dmhas

Connecticut NAMI www.namict.org

Connecticut 211 www.211ct.org

Delaware

Delaware Division of Substance Abuse and Mental Health www.dhss.delaware.gov/dsamh

Delaware NAMI www.namidelaware.org

Delaware 211 www.delaware211.org

Florida

Florida Department of Children and Families - Mental Health Services www.dcf.state.fl.us/programs/samh/mentalhealth

Florida NAMI www.namiflorida.org

Georgia

Georgia Department of Behavioral Health and Developmental Disabilities www.dbhdd.georgia.gov

Georgia NAMI www.namiga.org

Hawaii

State of Hawaii, Department of Health - Adult Mental Health Division www.health.hawaii.gov/amhd

Hawaii NAMI www.namihawaii.org

Hawaii 211 www.auw211.org

Idaho

Idaho Mental Health Services www.mentalhealth.idaho.gov

Idaho NAMI www.idahonami.org

Idaho 211 211.idaho.gov

Illinois

Illinois Department of Human Services - Mental Health www.dhs.state.il.us/page.aspx?item=29735

Illinois NAMI www.namiillinois.org

Illinois 211 www.illinois211.org

Indiana

Indiana Family and Social Services Administration www.in.gov/fssa/dmha

Indiana NAMI www.namiindiana.org

Indiana 211 www.in211.org

Iowa

Iowa Division of Mental Health and Disability Services www.dhs.iowa.gov/mhds

Iowa NAMI www.namiiowa.org

Iowa 211 www.211iowa.org

Kansas

Kansas Behavioral Health Services www.kdads.ks.gov/commissions/behavioral-health

Kansas NAMI www.namikansas.org

Kansas 211 www.unitedwayplains.org/2-1-1-landing-page

Kentucky

Kentucky Division of Behavioral Health www.dbhdid.ky.gov/dbh

Kentucky 211 www.uwky.org/211

Louisiana

Louisiana Department of Health - Office of Behavioral Health
www.ldh.la.gov/index.cfm/subhome/10

Louisiana NAMI www.namilouisiana.org

Louisiana 211 www.louisiana211.org

Maine

Maine Department of Health and Human Services - Substance Abuse and Mental Health Services www.maine.gov/dhhs/samhs

Maine NAMI www.namimaine.org

Maine 211 www.211maine.org

Maryland

Maryland Department of Health - Mental Health www.health.maryland.gov/ohcq/mh

Maryland NAMI www.namimd.org

Maryland 211 www.211md.org

Massachusetts

Massachusetts Department of Mental Health www.mass.gov/orgs/massachusetts-department-of-mental-health

Massachusetts Bureau of Substance Addiction Services www.mass.gov/orgs/bureau-of-substance-addiction-services

Massachusetts NAMI www.namimass.org

Massachusetts 211 www.mass211.org

Michigan

Michigan Department of Health and Human Services www.michigan.gov/mdhhs

Michigan NAMI www.namimi.org

Michigan 211 www.mi211.org

Minnesota

Minnesota Department of Human Services www.mn.gov/dhs/people-we-serve

Minnesota NAMI www.namihelps.org

Minnesota 211 www.211unitedway.org

Mississippi

Mississippi Department of Mental Health www.dmh.ms.gov

Mississippi NAMI www.namims.org

Mississippi 211 www.211ms.com

Missouri

Missouri Department of Mental Health www.dmh.mo.gov

Missouri NAMI www.namimissouri.org

Missouri 211 www.211helps.org

Montana

Montana Department of Health - Addictive and Mental Disorders dphhs.mt.gov/amdd

Montana NAMI www.namimt.org

Montana 211 www.montana211.org

Nebraska

Nebraska Department of Health and Human Services - Division of Behavioral Health www.dhhs.ne.gov/behavioral_health

Nebraska NAMI www.naminebraska.org

Nebraska 211 www.211iowa.org

Nevada

Nevada Division of Public and Behavioral Health www.dpbh.nv.gov

Nevada NAMI www.naminevada.org

Nevada 211 www.nevada211.org

New Hampshire

New Hampshire Department of Health and Human Services - Bureau of Behavioral Health www.dhhs.nh.gov/dcbcs/bbh

New Hampshire Department of Health and Human Services - Bureau of Drug and Alcohol Services www.dhhs.nh.gov/dcbcs/bdas

New Hampshire NAMI www.naminh.org

New Hampshire 211 www.211nh.org

New Jersey

New Jersey Integrated Health www.nj.gov/health/integrated-health

New Jersey NAMI www.naminj.org

New Jersey 211 www.nj211.org

New Mexico

New Mexico Human Service Department - Behavioral Health Services Division www.hsd.state.nm.us/Behavioral_Health_Services_Division.aspx

New Mexico Crisis Line www.nmcrisisline.com/resources

New Mexico NAMI www.naminewmexico.org

New York

New York State Office of Mental Health www.omh.ny.gov

New York State Office of Alcoholism and Substance Abuse Services www.oasas.ny.gov

New York NAMI www.naminys.org

New York City NAMI www.naminycmetro.org

New York 211 www.211nys.org

North Carolina

North Carolina Mental Health, Development Disabilities and Substance Abuse Services www.ncdhhs.gov/providers/provider-info/mh-dd-sas

North Carolina NAMI www.naminc.org

North Carolina 211 www.unitedwaync.org/nc211

North Dakota

North Dakota Behavioral Health Services www.nd.gov/dhs/services/mentalhealth

North Dakota NAMI www.namind.org

North Dakota 211 www.myfirstlink.org/services/2-1-1-helpline

Ohio

Ohio Mental Health and Addiction Services www.mha.ohio.gov

Ohio NAMI www.namiohio.org

Ohio 211 www.211oh.org

Oklahoma

Oklahoma Department of Mental Health and Substance Abuse Services www.ok.gov/odmhsas

Oklahoma NAMI www.namioklahoma.org

Oklahoma 211 www.211oklahoma.org

Oregon

Oregon Health Authority - Addiction and Mental Health Services www.oregon.gov/oha/hsd/amh/pages/index.aspx

Oregon NAMI www.namior.org

Oregon 211 www.211info.org

Pennsylvania

Pennsylvania Department of Human Services - Mental Health www.dhs.pa.gov/citizens/mentalhealthservices

Pennsylvania Department of Human Services - Substance Abuse Services www.dhs.pa.gov/citizens/substanceabuse-services

Pennsylvania NAMI www.namikeystonepa.org

Pennsylvania 211 www.pa211.org

Rhode Island

Rhode Island Department of Behavioral Healthcare, Developmental Disabilities and Hospitals www.bhddh.ri.gov

Rhode Island NAMI www.namirhodeisland.org

Rhode Island 211 www.uwri.org/get-help-2-1-1

South Carolina

South Carolina Department of Mental Health www.scdmh.net

South Carolina Department of Alcohol and Other Drug Abuse Services www.daodas.sc.gov

South Carolina NAMI www.namisc.org

South Carolina 211 www.sc211.org

South Dakota

South Dakota Division of Behavioral Health www.dss.sd.gov/behavioralhealth

South Dakota NAMI www.namisouthdakota.org

South Dakota 211 www.helplinecenter.org/2-1-1-community-resources

Tennessee

Tennessee Department of Mental Health and Substance Abuse Services www.tn.gov/behavioral-health

Tennessee NAMI www.namitn.org

Tennessee 211 tn211.mycommunitypt.com

Texas

Texas Health and Human Services - Mental Health and Substance Abuse Division www.dshs.texas.gov/mhsa-mh-help

Texas NAMI www.namitexas.org

Texas 211 www.211texas.org

Utah

Utah Department of Human Services - Substance Abuse and Mental Health www.dsamh.utah.gov

Utah NAMI www.namiut.org

Utah 211 www.211utah.org

Vermont

Vermont Department of Mental Health www.mentalhealth.vermont.gov

Vermont Alcohol & Drug Abuse www.healthvermont.gov/alcohol-drugs

Vermont NAMI www.namivt.org

Vermont 211 www.vermont211.org

Virginia

Virginia Department of Behavioral Health and Developmental Services www.dbhds.virginia.gov

Virginia NAMI www.namivirginia.org

Virginia 211 www.211virginia.org

Washington

Washington State Department of Social and Health Services www.dshs.wa.gov/bha

Washington NAMI www.namiwa.org

Washington 211 www.win211.org

West Virginia

West Virginia Bureau for Behavioral Health and Health Facilities www.dhhr.wv.gov/bhhf

West Virginia 211 www.wv211.org

Wisconsin

Wisconsin Department of Health Services - Mental Health Partner/Provider Resources www.dhs.wisconsin.gov/mh/dcindex.htm

Wisconsin NAMI www.namiwisconsin.org

Wisconsin 211 www.211wisconsin.org

Wyoming

Wyoming Department of Health - Behavioral Health Division www.health.wyo.gov/behavioralhealth

Wyoming NAMI www.namiwyoming.org

Wyoming 211 211wyoming.communityos.org

Washington DC

Washington DC Department of Behavioral Health www.dbh.dc.gov

DC NAMI www.namidc.org/home

Washington DC 211 www.211metrodc.org

GLOSSARY

You could go to grad school to understand what pros in the mental health care system are talking about. Or you could use this cheat sheet instead.

Acute: Severe and potentially short-term increase in symptoms.

Antidepressant: Prescription medication that treats symptoms of depression and anxiety.

Antipsychotic: Prescription medication that treats psychotic symptoms of mental illness.

Assessment: An appointment in which a healthcare provider asks a patient questions about their mental and physical health to determine treatment.

Case Manager: A health care provider who is primarily responsible for coordinating a patient's care, which may include social services.

Chronic: Illness that is expected to last a long time.

Comorbidity: Having two or more illnesses.

Confidential: Private information that is given to a provider and can only be shared with the patient's consent.

Consumer: Someone who uses health care services.

Crisis: Emotional, physical, or mental health emergency.

Crisis counseling: Short-term counseling that minimizes distress, provides emotional support, and immediate coping strategies.

Crisis hotline: Telephone, text, or chat service that provides free crisis counseling.

Diagnosis: The act of determining and describing a specific illness.

Disability: Limited ability to do daily activities.

Dual Diagnosis: Having a substance use disorder and a mental disorder at the same time.

Evidence-based practice: Treatments that have been proven effective by clinical research.

Inpatient: Someone who is admitted to a hospital or treatment facility, typically for an overnight stay.

Insight: Understanding one's own illness and symptoms.

Intervention: Strategy or treatment intended to improve the course of an illness.

Means: Objects used to cause violent or harmful acts (i.e., gun, knife, rope, poison).

Means restriction: Reducing access to means in an effort to prevent violence or harm.

Mental disorder: Illness characterized by impairing or altering a person's thoughts, moods, or behavior that causes distress or disability by disrupting normal thinking, feeling, and daily functioning.

Mental health: A state of mental and emotional wellbeing characterized by the absence of mental illness.

Mental health services: Health care designed to improve the mental health of patients.

Mental illness: See mental disorder.

Outpatient: Health care treatment that happens outside of a hospital or without an overnight stay.

Prevention: Activities to prevent the diagnosis or worsening of an illness.

Protective factors: Things that make it less likely that someone will develop a disorder.

Psychiatric disorder: See mental disorder.

Psychiatry: The branch of medicine that deals with the diagnosis and treatment of mental disorders.

Psychology: The science of human behavior.

Psychosis: When a person has lost touch with reality and cannot understand what is real and what is not.

Public health: The science and art of promoting health and preventing disease.

Recovery: When someone with a mental disorder is no longer dealing with symptoms and can resume their life.

Risk factors: Things that make it more likely that someone will develop a disorder.

Safety Plan: A plan designed to keep a person safe from self-harm or suicide.

Screening: A brief test to determine if someone is at risk for a disorder or illness.

Self-harm: Deliberately injuring oneself.

Serious mental illness: A disorder that causes severe impairment and limits one or more major life activities.

Stigma: A mark of disgrace that sets a person apart from others.

Suicidal ideation: Thinking about or planning one's suicide.

Suicide: Causing your own death on purpose.

Suicide attempt: Attempting to kill yourself.

Suicide attempt survivors: Someone who makes an attempt to kill themselves but does not die.

Suicide survivors: People with a loved one who has died by suicide.

Suicide warning signs: Indicators that someone is at risk for suicide.

Symptom: Physical or mental sign that indicates a disorder.

REFERENCES

In the era of fake news, it is important to know that I'm not making this stuff up. I've tried to cite every study, fact, and figure referenced. If you want to dig deeper into a certain topic, this is a good place to start. The complete list—including celebrity interviews about mental illness—are available at www.ashleyawomble.com.

Introduction

Key Substance Use and Mental Health Indicators in the United States: Results from the 2015 National Survey on Drug Use and Health. Rockville, MD: Substance Abuse and Mental Health Services Administration, 2016.

Part One: Choose Your Own Adventure

Cross-Disorder Group of the Psychiatric Genomics Consortium. "Identification Of Risk Loci With Shared Effects On Five Major Psychiatric Disorders: A Genome-Wide Analysis." *The Lancet*, 381, no. 9875 (February 2013).

Diagnostic and Statistical Manual of Mental Disorders: DSM-5. Arlington, VA: American Psychiatric Association, 2013.

Kessler, R., Chiu, W. Demler, O., and E. Walters. "Prevalence, Severity, and Comorbidity of 12-Month DSM-IV Disorders in the National Comorbidity Survey Replication." *Archives of General Psychiatry* 62, no. 6 (June 2005): 617-27. doi:10.1016/s0084-3970(08)70124-5.

Key Substance Use and Mental Health Indicators in the United States: Results from the 2015 National Survey on Drug Use and Health. Rockville, MD: Substance Abuse and Mental Health Services Administration, 2016.

Lieberman, Jeffrey A. *Shrinks: The Untold Story of Psychiatry.* London: Wiedenfeld & Nicolson, 2016.

Sederer, Lloyd I. *The Family Guide to Mental Health Care.* New York, NY: W.W. Norton & Company, 2015.

Understanding Mental Disorders: Your Guide to DSM-5. Arlington, VA: American Psychiatric Association, 2015.

Part Two: Master Your Mental Health Care

2015 National Survey on Drug Use and Health: Detailed Tables. Rockville, MD: Substance Abuse and Mental Health Services Administration. Center for Behavioral Health Statistics and Quality, 2016.

APA Presidential Task Force on Evidence-Based Practice. "Evidence-Based Practice in Psychology." *American Psychologist* (May/June 2006).

Kazdin, Alan E. *Encyclopedia of Psychology.* Oxford: Oxford Univ. Press, 2000.

Sederer, Lloyd I. *The Family Guide to Mental Health Care.* New York, NY: W.W. Norton & Company, 2015.

Stahl, Stephen M. *Stahl's Essential Psychopharmacology: Neuroscientific Basis and Practical Application.* Cambridge: Cambridge University Press, 2013.

"Types of Mental Health Professionals." Mental Health America. May 2018. www.mentalhealthamerica.net/types-mental-health-professionals.

Understanding Mental Disorders: Your Guide to DSM-5. Arlington, VA: American Psychiatric Association, 2015.

"Understanding Psychotherapy and How it Works." American Psychiatric Association. May 2018. www.apa.org/helpcenter/understanding-psychotherapy.aspx.

Part Three: All About the Bills

"Average Annual Single Premium per Enrolled Employee For Employer-Based Health Insurance." The Henry J. Kaiser Family Foundation. www.kff.org/other/state-indicator/single-coverage.

Coleman, Kev. "Aging Consumers without Subsidies Hit Hardest by 2017 Obamacare Premium & Deductible Spikes." Health Pocket. October, 26, 2016. www.healthpocket.com/healthcare-research/infostat/2017-obamacare-premiums-deductibles.

Claxton, C., Rae, M., Long, M., Damico, A., Whitmore, A., and G. Foster. "Health Benefits In 2017: Stable Coverage, Workers Faced Considerable Variation In Costs." *Health Affairs* 36, no. 10 (2017). doi: 10.1377/hlthaff.2017.0919.

"Glossary." U.S. Department of Health and Human Services. www.healthcare.gov/glossary.

"History of Health Reform Efforts in the United States." Kaiser Family Foundation. March 25, 2011. www.kff.org/health-reform/timeline/history-of-health-reform-efforts-in-the-united-states.

"Medicare and Mental Health." Center for Medicare Advocacy. May 2018. www.medicareadvocacy.org/medicare-and-mental-health/.

Medicare and Your Mental Health Benefits. Baltimore, MD: U.S. Department of Health and Human Services. Centers for Medicare & Medicaid Services. 2017.

Melek, S., Perlman, D., Davenport, S., Matthews, K. and M. Mager. *Impact of Mental Health Parity and Addiction Equity Act*. Milliman, 2017.

Moseley, G. "History of Medicine." *American Medical Journal of Ethics* 10, no 5 (May 2008).

Part Four: Be Kind to Your Body

Akbaraly, T., Brunner, E., Ferrie, J., Marmot, M., Kivimaki, M., and A. Singh-Manoux. "Dietary Pattern And Depressive Symptoms In Middle Age." *The British Journal of Psychiatry* 195, 5 (2009).

"Alcohol Use and Your Health." Centers for Disease Control and Prevention. January 3, 2018. www.cdc.gov/alcohol/fact-sheets/alcohol-use.htm.

Anglin, R., Z. Samaan, S. Walter, and S. McDonald. "Vitamin D Deficiency And Depression in Adults: Systematic Review and Meta-Analysis." *British Journal of Psychiatry* (2013). doi:10.1192/bjp.bp.111.106666.

Annual Surveillance Report of Drug-Related Risks and Outcomes — United States, 2017. Surveillance Special Report 1. Atlanta, GA: U.S. Department of Health and Human Services, Centers for Disease Control and Prevention. August 31, 2017.

Beirne, P., Clarkson, J., and H. Worthington. "Recall Intervals For Oral Health In Primary Care Patients." *Cochrane Database System Review* (2007). doi: 0.1002/14651858.CD004346.pub3.

Bridges, C. and T. Coyne-Beasley. "Advisory Committee On Immunization Practices Recommended Immunization Schedule for Adults Aged 19 Years or Older-United States, 2014." Centers for Disease Control and Prevention, Morbidity and Mortality Weekly Report. Atlanta, GA: February 3, 2014.

Bond, A. "Why Fentanyl Is Deadlier Than Heroin, In A Single Photo." Stat News. September 29, 2016. www.statnews.com/2016/09/29/fentanyl-heroin-photo-fatal-doses.

Cooney, G., Dwan, K., and G. Mead. "Exercise for Depression." *Journal of the American Medical Association* 311, 2432 (2014). doi:10.1001/jama.2014.4930.

Costandi, M. "A Brief History Of Psychedelic Psychiatry." The Guardian. September 2, 2014. www.theguardian.com/science/neurophilosophy/2014/sep/02/psychedelic-psychiatry.

"Diet is Associated with Risk of Depression." Science Daily. September 23, 2013. www.sciencedaily.com/releases/2013/09/130916103530.htm.

"Heroin." National Institute on Drug Abuse. January 2018. www.drug-abuse.gov/publications/research-reports/heroin.

Johns, A. "Psychiatric Effects of Cannabis." British Journal of Psychiatry 178, 2 (2001). doi:10.1192/bjp.178.2.116.

Lipari, R. and S. Van Horn. Smoking and mental illness among adults in the United States. Rockville, MD: Center for Behavioral Health Statistics and Quality, Substance Abuse and Mental Health Services Administration, March 30, 2017.

"Many Mental Illnesses Reduce Life Expectancy More Than Heavy Smoking." Science Daily. May 23, 2014. www.sciencedaily.com/releases/2014/05/140523082934.htm.

Miller, S. "Dangerous Drugs: Why Synthetic-Cannabinoid Overdoses Are On the Rise." Live Science. July 14, 2016. www.livescience.com/55406-synthetic-cannabinoids-overdoses-increasing.html.

Nardi, A., A. Valenca, I. Nascimento, R. Freire, A. Veras, V. De-Melo-Neto, F. Lopes, A. King, G. Soares-Filho, M. Mezzasalma, et al. "A Caffeine Challenge Test in Panic Disorder Patients, Their Healthy First-degree Relatives, and Healthy Controls." Depression and Anxiety 25, no. 10 (2008).

Nauert, R. "Dehydration Influences Mood, Cognition." Psych Central. psychcentral.com/news/2012/02/20/dehydration-influences-mood-cognition/35037.html.

Sifferlin, A. "13% of Americans Take Antidepressants." TIME. August 15, 2017. time.com/4900248/antidepressants-depression-more-common.

"Sleep and mental health." Harvard Medical School. July 2009. www.health.harvard.edu/newsletter_article/Sleep-and-mental-health.

"Synthetic Cannabinoids." National Institute on Drug Abuse. February 2018. www.drugabuse.gov/publications/drugfacts/synthetic-cannabinoids.

Treatment Improvement Protocol (TIP) Series, No. 33. Rockville, MD: Substance Abuse and Mental Health Services Administration, 1999.

Part Six: Find Your Purpose

"Depression, PTSD, & Other Mental Health Conditions in the Workplace: Your Legal Rights." U.S. Equal Employment Opportunity Commission. May 2018. www.eeoc.gov/eeoc/publications/mental_health.cfm.

"FMLA (Family & Medical Leave)." United States Department of Labor. May 2018. www.dol.gov/general/topic/benefits-leave/fmla.

"Monthly number of part-time employees in the United States from April 2017 to April 2018." Statista. May 2018. www.statista.com/statistics/192342/unadjusted-monthly-number-of-part-time-employees-in-the-us.

"Road to Recovery: Employment and Mental Illness" Washington, DC: National Alliance on Mental Illness. July 2014. www.nami.org/About-NAMI/Publications-Reports/Public-Policy-Reports/RoadtoRecovery.pdf.

Saks, E. "A Tale of Mental Illness From the Inside." Ted. June 2012. www.ted.com/talks/elyn_saks_seeing_mental_illness/transcript.

"Succeeding at Work." National Alliance on Mental Illness. May 2018. www.nami.org/Find-Support/Living-with-a-Mental-Health-Condition/Succeeding-at-Work.

Svoboda, E. "Hard-Wired for Giving." Wall Street Journal. August 31, 2017. www.wsj.com/articles/hardwired-for-giving-1377902081.

Part Eight: When It's Not You, It's...

Kessler, R., Amminger, G., Aguilar Gaxiola, S., Alonso, J., Lee, S., and T. Ustun. "Age of Onset of Mental Disorders: A Review of Recent Literature." *Current Opinion in Psychiatry* 20, 4 (2007). doi:10.1097/YCO.0b013e32816ebc8c.

Part Nine: Save Your Own Life

Addressing Suicidal Thoughts and Behaviors in Substance Abuse Treatment. Treatment Improvement Protocol (TIP) Series 50. Rockville, MD: Substance Abuse and Mental Health Services Administration, 2009.

Curtin, S., Warner, M., and H. Hedegaard. *Increase in suicide in the United States, 1999–2014. NCHS data brief, no 241.* Hyattsville, MD: National Center for Health Statistics, 2016.

National Strategy for Suicide Prevention: Goals and Objectives for Action. Washington DC: U.S. Department of Health and Human Services (HHS) Office of the Surgeon General and National Action Alliance for Suicide Prevention, 2012.

Stanley, B. and G. Brown. "Safety Planning Intervention: A Brief Intervention to Mitigate Suicide Risk." *Cognitive and Behavioral Practice* 19, 2 (2012).

"Suicide in America: Frequently Asked Questions." National Institute on Mental Health. May 2018. www.nimh.nih.gov/health/publications/suicide-faq.

"Suicide Prevention." National Institute on Mental Health. May 2018. www.nimh.nih.gov/health/topics/suicide-prevention.

ONE LAST THING

In this book, I've shared every way I know how to deal with mental illness. For most of us, it will take a combination of medication and therapy to get the symptoms under control. Then it's daily battle to make sure they don't show up again. Some days will feel like a fight, and occasionally you may lose. Keep going. You are worth the effort.

I hope you've been inspired by the people who shared their stories in this book. They have all been through dark days, but each of them found a way forward. I know that you can too.

No matter how much you are hurting or how much control you have lost over your thoughts and actions, it is possible to recover. There is no minimum amount of pain that you need to endure before you reach out for support.

You don't have to do this by yourself. There are so many smart and compassionate mental health professionals out there who want to help you. Medications and therapies now exist to treat even the most serious mental illnesses. There is one that will work for you.

You'll also need to show yourself a little love and patience. Learn to take care of your body and mind, and it will be easier to deal with everything else life throws at you. Lean on your loved ones, whether they are friends, family, or furry. Ignore the haters.

There may be moments when you feel like you can't deal with life anymore. You might think that the pain you feel will never end. Believe me, when I say it will.

You deserve to have an awesome life—and you can make it happen. Now that you know how to deal with your mental illness, you can take control of your health, your life, and your future.

Everything is going to be OK. You are going to make it happen.

Acknowledgments

This book would not be what it is without the brilliantly funny illustrations of Hillary Fitzgerald Campbell. If people only read this for the cartoons, they'd still get the point.

Thank you to my editor Laura Ross for being a champion of my writing since way back, and guiding me through this process with your sharp and swift edits. I'm grateful to the talented and patient Lauren Harms for making this book come to life with her savvy design skills. I'm also indebted to Rebecca Frumento, for being an early reader, fact checker, and working hard to create the resource guide.

Thanks to Dr. Ben Nordstrom and Dr. John Draper, both for lending your expertise to make sure this book is legit, and for the encouragement along the way. To everyone who shared their experiences with me, you'll never know thankful I am, or how much your stories mean to people who are struggling.

A big shout-out to my A-List: Claire Cuno, Sunitha Menon, Carole DiMarzo, Lidia Bernik, Gloria Dawson, and Erin

Quinn-Kong. I'm so grateful to have each of you in my life. And thanks to my family, for believing in me.

Thank you to my Phoenix House family for the encouragement along the way, especially Jana French, Christina DeGuardi, Sophie Forman, Genevieve Vaida, and Natalie Kuehn. I would be remiss not to mention John Searles, an author and mentor I admire deeply, who pushes me to keep writing.

Like so much in my life, this book came together thanks to love and support of my husband, Barry. Thank you for being my partner in life and everything else.

ABOUT THE AUTHOR

Ashley Womble is an award-winning journalist with a Masters in Public Health. Her mission is to change the way people think and talk about mental health. She lives in Brooklyn, New York. You can learn more about her at www.ashleyawomble.com.